326   6082

DISCARD

Remix

HENRY HOLT AND COMPANY . NEW YORK

Marina Budhos

Remix

conversations with immigrant teenagers

Henry Holt and Company, LLC
Publishers since 1866
115 West 18th Street
New York, New York 10011

Henry Holt is a registered trademark of Henry Holt and Company, LLC

Library of Congress Cataloging-in-Publication Data
Budhos, Marina Tamar.
Remix: conversations with immigrant teenagers / by Marina Budhos.
p.   cm.
Includes index.
Summary: Presents profiles of teenagers from countries
around the world, revealing their struggles to fit into American
society and their personal triumphs.
1. Children of immigrants—United States—Interviews.
2. Teenagers—United States—Interviews.   [1. Immigrants—
Interviews.]   I. Title.
JV6600.B83   1999   920'.00835—dc21   [B]   99-25266

ISBN 0-8050-5113-9
First Edition—1999
Printed in the United States of America
on acid-free paper. ∞
1 3 5 7 9 10 8 6 4 2
Book design by Debbie Glasserman

To those teenagers who have arrived
and those who have yet to arrive

There are many people who have helped me in researching this book. Thanks to:

Jay Cohen and Cornelia Gutwein at Flushing High School; Lydia Nagel, for her unflagging commitment to the project; Shel Erlich of the Los Angeles United School District; Carol Truscott and Nancy Ritter of Fairfax High School; Bud Jacobs of Venice High School; Maria Olmos of the Newcomer's Center in Belmont High School; Rajini Srikanth, who pointed me to Sonia Aurora, who led me to Sandra Canas at Cambridge Community Services; Eliza Dresang and Lao Pao Vang in Madison, Wisconsin; Gauitra Bahadur, for decisive leads; Danny Kessler at Prospect Heights High School.

Sunaina Maira, for her insightful conversations; Somini Sengupta, for her excellent reporting that led me to the concept of remix; Shirley Budhos, for entry to Flushing High School; Ed Rothfarb and Peter Trias, for a resting place in Los Angeles; Kim Vaeth, and Sanjay and Vibha Nigam, for home bases in a blustery Boston; Maricel Presilla, for her island of Cuba in Hoboken, New Jersey.

My husband, Marc Aronson—editor, collaborator, and partner in all things that matter—who listened and nudged me along.

And finally, thank you to all the teenagers for trusting me and sharing their stories.

Contents

Remix

Introduction

The school halls are paved with gold

On a cold spring day, I emerge from the subway in Queens, New York, and step into my old teenage life.

Standing at the main intersection in downtown Flushing, I see the army-navy store where, in the 1970s, I bought my cargo pants and construction boots, the department store where I once was caught shoplifting, the fuddy-duddy nurse's-uniform store and Peck's Office Supply Shop where even then everything seemed preserved from decades before. Farther up Main Street I can see the building where I took a driver's-education class, that most precious pass to teenage freedom.

I have also arrived in a strange and unfamiliar place. A clutter of signs in Korean advertise banks, restaurants, clothing stores, insurance companies. The hot-dog and pizza places are now bakeries selling flaky buns filled with sweet red-bean paste, or noodle houses with glazed chickens hanging from hooks in the window; the jewelry stores display gleaming, green jade bangles. An elderly Asian couple argue on a corner; glamorous young women show me Shiseido makeup in an indoor shopping plaza selling only Asian foods. Most of the faces are Asian, though I see black and Latino people descend into the subway, get on the buses. I remember how, when my father and I used to walk on Main Street, we were often the only Asian-looking people in a crowd.

I am the child of two different streams of immigration. On one side, my Russian Jewish grandparents were part of the immigration wave that ended in 1924, when the National Origins Act created ethnic quotas and severely limited immigration from southern and Eastern Europe, Asia, and Africa. My grandmother fled her small town outside Kiev to work illegally in a laundry in Europe before coming to New York, where she married her first cousin. I grew up with stories about the first day my grandmother went to work in a factory. The trains broke down and she had to walk across Brooklyn Bridge, not knowing a word of English, carrying only a nickel in her pocket. My grandmother went to night school, but she never fully learned English. She used to send me cards from Brooklyn written in a childish scrawl. To her, the nearby borough of Queens was off the edge of the earth, as far away as America was to her when she was in Russia.

My father came from British Guiana after World War II as a college scholarship student. As a man of Indian descent from the Caribbean, he was not eligible to immigrate to the United States. He only became an American citizen because he married my mother, an American woman. When he began to work as a teacher in a Queens high school, he was the first Indian or Caribbean on the faculty.

With its ribbons of wide-lane avenues unfurling toward the Long Island suburbs, Queens was an in-between place, a stopover on the way to the real America. For a teenager in the seventies, it was bleached jeans, Farrah Fawcett hairdos, disco, fast-food restaurant jobs, Camaro cars. The residential streets of brick and shingle houses were parceled into Irish and Italian Catholic, Greek, Jewish neighborhoods.

Racially it was divided too, with Jamaica Avenue the dividing axis that separated north from south, white from black, with some mixture in between. Flushing was most definitely on the northern, white side.

Queens is now a lively immigrant borough, the most diverse area in the United States, and a microcosm of the varied landscape of immigrant America. Here you can find working-class immigrant neighborhoods crowded with shops selling Dominican *café con leche* and Indian sari stores; tough urban streets known for drug trafficking and gangs; tree-lined roads where immigrants have bought comfortable houses within a short time of their arrival. These are the many forms of the new immigration: Some newcomers were professionals in their countries and settled in the United States with barely a ripple of economic adjustment. They live in suburbs, drive new cars, and have immediately become part of the American middle class. Some have already lived and worked in other countries, and bring over a sense of savvy and entrepreneurial zeal in coping with a new culture. Others have landed in a ghetto, where their children easily join America's marginalized poor.

Up ahead, on a slight rise, is Flushing High School, where my own mother taught for several years. It is a huge, hulking castle of a building with turrets and stained-glass windows. Once inside, I am shot back into familiar sensations: the halls painted in thick prison-gray; the swinging doors and huge windows that require a giant pole to be opened; the kids shouting in the echoey, cage-wire stairwells. Then the loudspeaker lets out that all-too-familiar drone-blast announcing the next period.

Suddenly I am swept into a crush of people that resembles a New York City rush hour. Students flock out of classrooms, jostle through the swinging doors, up and down the stairwells. I am on a two-lane highway of backpacks and baggy jeans, as everyone shouts to friends in the opposite lane. Elbows, feet nudge me along; boys twist off girls' bag straps or flash hand signals to other boys. I can barely see where I am going. The noise is deafening.

I find the school bewildering. Even though I went to a similar city high school, I can't imagine how young people, much less immigrant teenagers, carve a niche for themselves in this noisy, congested place. There's no room, anywhere. The teachers have no private areas; they double and triple up on offices. No matter where you go, there's a clamor of voices.

This is the high school of today. Not only are we in the midst of a great immigrant wave, but we are experiencing the largest immigrant teenage population ever. More and more families immigrate when their children are on the cusp of adolescence. Or a parent will come first, and send for a son or daughter once the child becomes a teenager, so that he or she can continue studying and go on to college. And, as the *New York Times* has reported, many teenagers are coming here on their own.

In the old days, the expression was, "In America, the streets are paved with gold." Immigrants streamed into factories and shops, hoping to be among those who went from rags to riches. One of the myths about the early immigration is that all these immigrants dutifully sat at school desks and learned English. Most immigrants were actually very resistant to education. Their community leaders fought against a secular education, fought being Americanized and losing their language. Immigrant families needed their kids to work in the store or the factory or to peddle newspapers. Very few immigrant children finished high school. Girls, especially, received very little education. Those who stayed in school were the children of the middle class—doctors, professionals.

Today, it's the school halls that are paved with gold. Every September, families from all corners of the earth show up at schools to register their children. "I have come here for education, opportunity," they all say. They hope that school will magically transform an immigrant child from being the son of a maid, or the daughter of a factory worker, into part of the American middle class. And their focus on education is realistic: unlike turn-of-the-century immigrants, today's immigrants need a very high level of literacy and skills to function and move up in the American economy. These teenagers are the vessels of their parents' hopes and expectations; in turn, they are shaping our future. Schools like Flushing High have become the great swelling, overflowing, jammed highways that are carrying young people into America.

For the last two and a half years, I have been talking to immigrant teenagers all over the country, in Brooklyn and Queens, New York; Jersey City, New Jersey; Madison, Wisconsin; Cambridge, Massachusetts; and Los Angeles, California. Out of these conversations came a swirl of voices—voices that have so much to tell us.

Most of the immigrants I spoke to turned out to be older teenagers. Part of this is because immigrant teenagers tend to stay in school a little longer than other students. But more importantly, I found that the younger teenagers were not at the point where they could explain what had happened to them. By the time they were eighteen and nineteen, on the cusp of adulthood, they were creating the stories of their lives.

Immigrant teenagers speak not only about themselves but about the America they are immigrating into. They are like anthropologists who observe the codes of a strange new culture. What might be invisible to a native-born American teenager looms large and impenetrable to an immigrant teenager. Much of what defines American teenage life may be impossible for an immigrant teenager: dating, hanging out with friends, even choosing one's own friends. On the other hand, sometimes immigrants can take for granted things Americans might not know: extended families who watch over them, traditional mothers who egg them on; a church, a temple, a cohesive neighborhood or community.

All the teenagers I met were astonished by how independent American teenagers are, and amazed at how little respect they show to grown-ups. In a Brooklyn classroom, a girl from Grenada remarked, "In our country if your socks fell down on your ankles you'd get hit." Another girl, from Nigeria, chimed in that the same thing would get you ten lashes on your back in her country. "You have more freedom here," a Jamaican boy said. "But sometimes it's too much." Back home, no one would dream of talking back to a teacher. These kids are surprised by how easy American teenagers have it—especially when it comes to education. "We pay for everything in Grenada—our books, everything. Maybe education shouldn't be free; then they wouldn't take it for granted so much."

I found that most girls—though not all—are being pushed toward education and professions by their parents. For instance, three of the girls I interviewed were well on their way to becoming doctors, something that would have been unheard of at the turn of the century. There is Lucy, who, three years after coming from Korea, has entered a premed program; Farida, from Bangladesh, and Reshmee, a young Guyanese, will soon follow on a similar track. These girls are exceptional not only because they are achieving at such a high level, but because they often must balance very heavy pressures within their families. They are expected to be dutiful daughters, and they must fight and compete in the outside world. The pressure, Lucy confided to me, sometimes made her "sick in my mind."

Not all the teenagers I interviewed are model immigrants zooming to the top of the economic ladder. Many come from very poor countries, where they have spent very little time in school. Some can barely write, and they struggle to function at the level needed for living in the United States today. A teacher from Senegal who runs a special orientation program for recent immigrants told me how a full third of the students who come into his high school do not really know what it means to sit in a classroom. "We need civics," he claims. "We need to teach them how to be in this society."

Many immigrants have entered the neglected margins of American society, neighborhoods where the native-born have been struggling against their own descent into illiteracy, drugs, and chronic poverty. Immigrants, by virtue of their pluck and resistance, their determination to make themselves over, can overcome terrifying obstacles. But some of the teenagers I met stray. There is Hector from Guatemala, who joined a gang because it was too lonely in the apartment with his mother working all the time. Herman, a mixed-race boy from Guyana, took a zigzag path from gangsta rap to pop music. And others who do not even make it into a classroom are stuck in a grinding cycle of low-wage jobs.

Immigrant teenagers' lives can be marked by extremes: too much and too little community; too much and too little family. Unlike the turn of the century, when immigrants crammed into neighborhoods such as New York City's boisterous Lower East Side, immigrants can now be spread out across anonymous cities and suburban belts. Some teenagers come to live with parents who are complete strangers to them. Sorianyi, from Cambodia, arrived in the United States to find that her estranged father had a new family whom he no longer lived with, and he expected her to take care of him. Several of the teenagers I interviewed wound up on the streets or in shelters.

At the same time, immigrant teens are often answerable to a community that watches their every move like a gossipy village. A girl's reputation is the reputation of her family, the symbol of their purity in the face of America's contaminating influences. Girls' lives can turn very extreme and stark if they dare disobey their parents' wishes, especially when it comes to sex and boys. They become pariahs, sluts, disgraces to their family and community. There is Ashrat, disappearing from classes into the arms of a married man. There is Maria, uprooted from the Dominican Republic to live with a father she barely knows, moving from one boy to the next.

Since political and ethnic tensions overseas often don't register on American radar screens, immigrant teenagers find themselves wedged together with those from similar regions in groupings such as Latino or South Asian or Caribbean. Yet their home countries may be rivals or even enemies. At a Brooklyn high school I heard stories of Haitian young people being the target of insults from Jamaicans. A teasing match between Pakistani and Indian teenagers soon turned to nationalist insults. On the other hand, new friendships can bridge old chasms, for these young people are united in being immigrants trying to gain a toehold in an alien environment.

Immigrant teenagers often don't have any in-between space where they can work out the pressures of their in-between lives. School offers the only life they can have separate from their families, since they can't take for granted the casual hanging out and dating that's such a normal part of American teenage life. Many also have after-school jobs, which offer a buffer zone where they can learn to interact with Americans.

How do these young people place themselves in the fragmented racial map of America? I found that teenagers who had come over recently were not that interested in racial or ethnic distinctions. Yet, the longer an immigrant teenager has been in the country, the more aware he or she was of racial and ethnic codes. Some experienced outright harassment or discrimination. Those who were closer to second generation thought of themselves as Asian Americans or Latinos, for instance. They had a much stronger sense of "us" and "them," both as ethnics in white America and as young people against parents.

Unlike the previous wave of immigrants, these newcomers are fitting into a country where urban black culture is in popular movies, music, sports, billboards, clothing, TV ads. Some might mimic black hip-hop style—baggy pants, hand signals, and slang—as a way of expressing some American-style coolness. But underneath these gestures, most steer clear of too much racial mixing. Their prejudices, particularly against African Americans, are often reinforced by their parents. This can become especially complicated for immigrants from Africa or the Caribbean who are seen as American blacks but might identify with their own culture. As newcomers are being Americanized, they are becoming part of America's black and white split.

Where, then, is the great multicultural society that our demographics promise? I see it in the entry points—the English-as-a-second-language (ESL) classes where immigrant teenagers are thrust together with others who struggle with the same difficulties. There, the sense of sharing experiences is very powerful. I see it among the students chosen for elite academic programs, the athletes who compete in sports teams, or the techies who play video and computer games together. They transcend the cultural boundaries that define other young people. I saw it, too, in a church where a Haitian girl who ran away from an abusive aunt found hope and sustenance in the Church of Christ. There, she found community with other teenagers from all over the world.

If teenagers today live in small immigrant villages, they are also part of the larger global village. They all are touched, to some degree, by the same media world of TV, CDs, Internet, and advertisements. In an age of easy airplane travel and international phone lines, immigrants are able to keep up strong ties to their homelands. Caribbean young people go home in the summers to visit their grandparents. A young man from Delhi can go back in search of a bride in an arranged marriage. Assimilation has become more of a mingling, a back-and-forth process.

In music, a remix is a composite of different musical styles. Multitracks stretch familiar musical styles into hybrid sounds. The percussive beat of a Punjabi folk tune is grafted onto hip-hop or rap lyrics to make bhangra. Cape Verdean lyrics are mingled with the sweet rhythms of a Caribbean soca song. These teenagers I met are creating their own remix, piecing together the ruptures and pain, the challenges and excitement of their journeys. This book is itself a mix, composed of fourteen in-depth profiles alternated with short voice pieces. When the interviews are taken together, you can hear the mingled, syncopated melody of these young people's lives. They are all here, waiting to tell their stories, waiting to be heard.

Herman

Nineteen years old

"I came over here to become somebody, not to throw away my life in the gutter."

To visit Herman, I set off on what felt like an odyssey: the subway to the train to downtown Jersey City, where I picked up a bus that wound through different neighborhoods. When I was growing up, Jersey City was a working-class area that had fallen on rough times. During the early eighties, racial tensions ran high, and immigrant Indians became targets of violent attacks. As I emerged from the train station, I saw old skyscrapers whose peeling and faded insurance signs recall another era, when Jewish immigrants made their home here. Now a new wave of immigrants have reclaimed the streets and stores. Taking the bus down Union Avenue, I passed storefronts advertising overseas phone calls, Hispanic bakeries, Arabic shops selling figs and flatbreads. It was like going into deeper and deeper rings of change, watching as the city was transformed by each new immigrant group.

Herman, I learned, has gone through his own journey, traveling through different layers of American society since he arrived five years ago. Slender, with light-caramel skin and short cropped hair, Herman is hard to place ethnically, and soon it became clear that he has gone through many restless shifts in defining who he is.

Herman

Born in Amsterdam, Herman is of mixed descent; his mother is Indo-Guyanese and his father, who died when he was two, was English. Herman grew up in the rural Berbice region of Guyana, reared by his mother and stepfather. When his stepfather immigrated to the United States, Herman lost yet another childhood father figure. Fourteen when he arrived in this country, he found himself in search of a new self.

"It was hard," he said of his first months in the States. We were sitting in his parents' house, the clean, well-ordered home of proud immigrants, crowded with shiny brass tables, a synthetic zebra-striped rug, carefully arranged mementos. The entire time we talked, the television was on with the sound muted; the blinds and curtains were drawn.

"Soon as I'm settling down to get to know everybody to feel comfortable, I got to move to the high school; I'm like, Wow, I can't handle this. You got to watch out. They fight a lot there, they kill people, they get you scared. And when you go into the class, you're lost, it's a strange environment, here's big strong kids, looking at you. It was hard, very hard. I didn't have an older brother, I had to learn all by myself."

"What was the hardest thing to pick up on?"

"The people. Some could be real pains, they pick on you for no reason at all, just because if your clothes doesn't look like theirs."

Herman wanted to learn the code. In a tough place like Jersey City, known for its gangs and drugs, the testy violence between ethnic and racial groups, the question was, what does a half-Indo-Guyanese, half-English boy who could pass for being Hispanic become? Where does he fit in? Where in the racial map does he place himself?

Herman is always looking for the right look to slip into.

He played "homeboy," and went deep into rap music, imitating the tough kids he saw hanging out at school. Though he'd learned all the right cues, underneath he knew he was drifting.

"I used to listen to a lot of rap music, used to get into a whole vibe. I started dressing gangster-style, homeboy-style, my pants all the way down. I had to do it for, like, the freshman year. My uncle, they come around, sayin', 'What the hell are you wearing? What is that, man?' I don't pay no mind to them. I wasn't going to tell them what was going on, I was keeping it to myself."

One day, Herman was doing his laundry in his apartment building when a man began talking to him in Spanish. Because of his looks, this was something that often happened to Herman. Sometimes he didn't bother to correct the mistake; this time, he explained that he wasn't Latino, and the two began to talk. The man's name was Nico, and he was a twenty-seven-year-old father of two. Something in Herman must have moved the older man, who took him in, and began to guide him as a mentor.

"My whole life start changing rapidly. He showed me a different way. He said, 'Like the clothes you're wearing—people will think less of you.' I wasn't even thinking about that. I was trying to fit in. He started teaching me stuff, sayin', 'Stop hanging out with those kind of people. If you dress that way, people will think you're a gangster; that's not the image you want to project. You want to project something, for people to see you for what you are.' He took me shopping; first place we go, went there, we gonna get that, we gonna get that. He change me over."

It took a while, but Herman began to transform. His clothes, his outlook changed. He stopped wearing baggy clothes and put on straight jeans. He went with Nico to barbecues, family events. For six weeks, Nico trained him in self-defense moves, which he once used to quiet a guy who was bugging him in the back of the class. "I put a wedge between me and rap music. I just grab all the tapes and cut them up. Get rid of them, get rid of the image I had."

In school, he stayed quiet, stayed out of fights. The new Herman was a wholesome, tough, Clint Eastwood, survivalist man who relied on self-control. It gave him an edge over the other kids, and allowed him to remain separate and aloof.

"He was raisin' me up when he put all that stuff in my head. The kids, it's like I'm lookin' down on them and I'm on a higher level." He admitted he doesn't have any friends in school, because they're always getting high or stealing. "That's not my thing. I came over here to become somebody, not to throw away my life in the gutter." He avoided all groups—the Spanish kids, the black kids, the other Guyanese, for whom he reserves the most scorn.

"These kids, they want to be down with the homeboys, so they're throwing all their life away, smoking weed, hanging out drinking, cursing, having a kid on the corner, doin' this, doin' that. Here it is, their mom is at home trying to make a better life for them and they're out there screwin' it up. She doesn't know what's goin' on out here. When she finds out is when the cops call her up. Then it's sad. Here your mom's doin' so much for you and now she got to bail you out of jail because you screwed up."

Just when he got a firm grasp on this new Herman, his life was once more disrupted. His parents moved into a new house, and Nico was no longer nearby to guide him. Herman quickly began scouting for the next mentor. This one arrived in the guise of Eric, a man in his forties who strolled by one winter day as Herman was shoveling snow. The two struck up a friendship, and as Herman explained, "he became my new teacher."

"He started teaching me stuff from a different level. He's into the club scene, fast environment, music, a lot of high people, big people in big places. So I was like, Wow, so I got to deal with this now. He takes me to this club in New York and we spend the night here, coming home at two in the morning. He teach me stuff. When you go to a club, you can't do this, you can't do that.

"The other day, he told me, You got to change the way you dress. So I'm changing the way I'm dressed. He's putting me into suits, slacks, ties. The reason he's doin' this is he's hanging out with wealthy people. You got to dress to fit their standard. 'Cause they're always dressin' with suits, slacks, and that kinda look."

The room was growing darker and darker as Herman talked; ghostly MTV images flashed on the screen. I almost said something about turning on a light, then stopped myself. Herman, I saw, was a chameleon, who moved between different realities, first a rapper, then a cool proud man, now at home in the smoky blue chambers of clubs. His speech was coming on faster and faster, in a dreamy flow. He was proud, cocky, his talk a mix of rapture and scorn.

"Here I'm getting to meet people you see on TV—that's awesome, man. What young kid wouldn't want to do that? Not everybody would get to shake somebody's hand like that. You got to go through a mob of crowds and here your table's right here. And you're sittin' right next to the person and you're talking to them and they're asking you questions and you're answering and you're like, Hmm, man this is amazing stuff. So I'm gettin' the hang of this. I have my new teacher, I'm lovin' this."

"Now that I'm in this world, back at school, everything the kids do there is immature stuff. I don't want to be a part of that, that's whacked. Here, now, I'm thinkin' like a thirty-year-old, doin' stuff that a thirty-year-old would do, and my peers, they're like not even close, they're like way back. Here I'm chillin' in the classroom, thinking about where I went last night, who I hanged out with. They would go crazy if they knew I been there. Not everybody get a chance to hang out with a star."

His new "teacher" was leading him straight into the blue-light dream of media and music. One night Herman had a flash of inspiration. He realized he wanted to be a performer. "I want to create my own kind of music that nobody's ever heard of. If I die, they'll know, 'Oh, that guy, he created that music.'" His fantasy even seems predestined: in his childhood he always loved his huge speakers that made "you feel your heart going whoosh." His dead father, as it turns out, used to work as a deejay.

"It's in my blood, and the club has more technology. You got laser beams, the scene is so fast, everything is moving so fast, all the deejays—I'm hooked in. This is the new thing, this is the label, this is the market, makin' this much money.

"My friend, he brought me into this world, but now I'm driftin' away from him because he's more into the party kind of thing. So I'm moving up from there, getting to the deejays, hanging the whole time there, learning everything about the music, the synthesizers, all the equipment you can learn about, because I'm digging this stuff."

He and his friends plan to produce "pop-reggae" for the United States. Like Herman, this music would be a hybrid—reggae, with lyrics written and sung in standard English. For so many immigrant teenagers, music, TV, and movies are their entry into America. The media blur cultural boundaries, absorbing new influences at a dizzying speed. And immigrant teenagers can join in by watching TV, buying CDs, and going to dance clubs. They can move into

America faster than they might in other parts of their lives. Popular culture is the space where they can re-create themselves.

The steps ahead for making Herman's new music were vague: he mentioned possible voice lessons and writing songs, though he admitted he can't express what he means. He saw his break into the music world as a series of crafty, deliberate moves; he needs to "sneak" the sound into the industry, much the way he's learned to work around the bureaucracy at his high school to get the schedules he wants. When I pressed him on what he knew about synthesizers, he brought me into his bedroom to show me his music magazines, *GQ*, and *Esquire*. I'm not sure if Herman's talk is a fantasy that will evaporate tomorrow or a solid path into the future. It's too soon to tell. All I know is that through music Herman believes he can go deeper into America, deeper into his dreams. He seems to live in a netherworld of hope and confidence, always led by a new father figure into the next discovery.

At the end of the interview, I heard only his voice, a wild, dreamy riff. The television, eerily huge, showed a music video of waiflike girls in bathtubs, crouched in closets, their skin luminescent, like that of dolphins. I couldn't tell what was real, who Herman had become. "Are you American?" I asked. "I'm in between," he replied. "Deep down inside, where I was born, that's what I am. You can't change a tiger stripe." By this time, I couldn't find Herman. It was completely dark, and I couldn't see his face.

Lucy

Nineteen years old

"I'm their only hope."

"I'm their only hope," Lucy says bluntly. "My parents are Asian people. They want me to be a really great person. They have a lot of expectations of me. Almost perfect, good daughter and good sister, someone who has strong beliefs. I must be responsible. Obey. Take care of my brother for study. Give him advice."

Lucy is a heavyset, serious girl, considered one of the star students at Flushing High School in New York City. She will attend a premed program at the highly competitive SUNY Binghamton. Underneath her drive, though, is a grave intensity and a brooding air. I can feel the weight of responsibility she carries on her shoulders. And the more I talked to Lucy, the more I realized how much darkness and despair is inside her.

Lucy spoke slowly, and carefully considered her words, since English is still a struggle for her. She likes to tell a story about when she was growing up in Korea: Each time something good happened to Lucy, her grandfather appeared in her mother's dreams. Then her grandfather fell very sick, and her mother was often away, tending to him. A lonely Lucy stopped working hard in school. On the night her grandfather died, he appeared in Lucy's dream.

Lucy

She took that as a sign. It was time to be mature, to take responsibility for herself. From then on, everything in her life became a test of character. She studied hard, striving to be the perfect child her parents wanted.

Lucy came over from Korea with her brother and mother when she was sixteen years old to join her father, who had settled in the United States a few years before. Like many immigrant families, they decided to come here for their children's education and future.

But the immigration has been very hard. Lucy barely knows her father, who had always worked abroad. And to start over at the age of sixteen in a language she barely knew grated on Lucy's perfectionism. "I was always good at expressing my feelings and my thoughts to others. And suddenly, even though I want to say something, I can't. I'm stuck to express my feeling and my thoughts. It was a really big stress."

"Was your family having a lot of stress too?"

"In my country, Korea, my mom, my brother, and I, we were strongly bonding. Since we came here, I feel we are breaking up. Because my mom was in this problem, my brother in that problem. We don't have enough time to care for others. And I always keep my problems in my mind. I never said my problems or conflicts to my mom or brother. I couldn't." She sighed. "It was like habit. When I was young, my mom raise us by herself. I always try to keep my problem to myself. I don't want to put it on her.

"The worst enemy is myself," she explains. "Sometimes I'm disappointed with myself. That's the worst thing. Like when I didn't try to do my best. In school and in family."

There's a depth to Lucy. Each life obstacle, each difficulty, has become a spiritual lesson for her. She is obviously successful, but that's never enough. She has a restless, thoughtful air, as if she is always uncovering the hidden meaning behind any event. She scrutinizes herself, her family, those around her. This is also what propels her toward achievement, for she is never satisfied with a simple answer.

She told me yet another story: When she was very young, she fell sick for a long time. After she finally recovered, she had gained a lot of weight. Back at school, the other children relentlessly teased her. "I got upset, and because of that I got more mature than at the same age of the other kids. I got hurt by them. My mom, she really push me hard, she always wants me to be strong. Because my external appearance is not as good as others, I try to be an excellent person in my mind. I feel I'm really different. Internally. They are just kids, they don't understand. I spend more time reading a book, rather than playing with the same-age girls or boys. I get more intelligent than the others. I'm better than them."

Behind the strong, stoic front, though, was a childlike hope, a wish to be accepted like any other person. Respect, she hoped, would earn her a way out of the shame and hurt of being different. "If I try to study hard and I become a better person than them, maybe they will not tease me anymore."

Lucy described a very regimented life here in the United States. Her parents work long hours at a restaurant. Her mother is gone from ten in the morning until ten at night; usually she fixes dinner and leaves it for the children. After school, Lucy is responsible for cleaning the house. "It is my duty," she explained. Then she studies and watches her younger brother, who is now fifteen. Her brother has not been doing so well since he came here, which has added to her pressures. "He has problems. He's not as good at school. My parents are always comparing: I am so good, my brother is bad. Because of puberty, he made bad friends, I think. He's making trouble."

So much of her life is bound up in obligations and expectations that she feels she might explode. The pressure got especially bad a year and a half ago, and she became "sick in my mind, physically and mentally. I had stress and problems and I got really stressed and make ulcer."

That was when she met her best friend, another Korean girl. Lucy loves to talk about this girl—it is the only time she relaxes and giggles and her air of graveness lifts. Every afternoon, she and her friend go to Dunkin' Donuts, where, she explained, they "talk about life, what I feel. Sometimes I feel so good, sometimes I don't feel so good. I need a friend. I like her so much because she always listens to me and understands me. When I feel lonely and depressed she encourages me."

This friendship is Lucy's only bit of freedom, the place where she is not being a dutiful daughter, sister, student, translator, or model immigrant. There is little room for most immigrant girls to deviate from their parents' traditional expectations. Friendship is one place where they can let off a little steam, be themselves. "Asian and Korean parents more stick together with their children," Lucy explained. "American parents like the children to be more independent."

For Lucy, after a long childhood of staying separate from other children, feeling superior and more mature, her new friendship felt especially satisfying. She was catching up on everything she had missed out on in Korea: giggling, confidences, secrets. For once she could be young and uninhibited; she was finally herself, not the sum of her family's expectations.

But then Lucy's friendship sparked the biggest conflict in her life. Her mother did not approve of the other girl, who hadn't finished high school and works in a bakery.

"Since I was a little child, in elementary school, junior-high school, high school, my mom still pushing me. About friends. Studying. I always follow what she said. But right now, I should follow the things that are right. I still make my own friend."

On our second meeting, I arranged to meet Lucy at the same Dunkin' Donuts. It was a hot day, and the walk from the subway took much longer than I expected. Lucy, who was waiting, seemed surprised by my lateness. I sensed something had shifted. There was an urgency to our meeting. She was depending more on this interview; she had more to tell me. I also felt I had let her down. Lateness is something that she simply does not tolerate in herself or anyone else.

Lucy had brought many snapshots from her childhood to show me, and spread them out on the table. Most of them were of birthdays and graduations. There was young Lucy dressed up in a traditional outfit, surrounded by elaborate cut-paper decorations and neat pyramids of oranges and apples. Even then she looked thoughtful and serious. In all the pictures, her mother hovers nearby. Perhaps most telling was the picture of her junior-high graduation: with outstretched arms, she hands a bouquet of flowers to her mother, who blushes and looks shyly at the ground. It is a gesture of daughterly gratitude, while her mother humbly refuses the honor.

Here in Dunkin' Donuts, far away from Korea, Lucy quickly launched into a long, unhappy outpouring about her mother. Since I had last seen her, the conflict had reached a breaking point. One night, her mother forbade Lucy to see her friend. During the fight, her mother hit her, something that had never before happened. Worse yet, her mother said that if Lucy dared to meet with her friend she would have to leave home. "If you're going to follow your own rule," she told her, "get out of here."

Typically, Lucy saw this conflict as another test of her character. "I got really upset. But I didn't cry in front of her. I'm very strong in controlling my feelings."

Her tone became more exasperated and outraged as she sorted through her tumble of emotions and newfound beliefs. "I should decide which friend is good for me. Not my mom. She should not decide about that anymore, that's what I think. My mom gets really, really upset at that concept. My mom thinks I'm still young and not an experienced person about life, that I'm really stupid because I'm not following her rule. I try to have a nice conversation with her and I try to persuade her. But it was really, really hard."

"What does your friend think?"

"She's great. When I told her about this, my friend told me that, even though your mom did do bad things to you, she is still your mother. I can't betray you. But your mom, she's not going to betray you, so you should follow your mom."

It was a remarkable moment—two Korean girls struggling to be independent while staying loyal to their parents. The very rules that are driving them apart actually brought them closer together, since they share this same respect for their elders. Two American girls might well unite against a strict mom.

"She's so nice," Lucy added. "She told me, Let's cut down on our meeting and just try to hide from sight."

Lucy had entered a kind of half-world made up of both rebellion and dutifulness. She and her friend schemed up various ways to see one another on the sly. Lucy's mother's power over her had diminished. She admitted, uncomfortably, that she had been lying and dismissed her mother's threats to go to the other girl's mother as "nonsense."

Beneath her strong defiance, Lucy longed for something else, something new. Her friendship had opened the door to

American-style confession and intimacy. Lucy spoke of "independence," of "a space which is my own." Accustomed now to sharing her feelings, she began to pressure her mother to give her a kind of support unheard of in Korea.

"It is my parents, because they are Korean, because of culture, they don't express their feelings or thoughts very often. My mom never gave me a compliment. But I'm still a human being. I need to hear, 'Oh, you're good.' My mom is proud of me, she believes me, that's why she doesn't express. I know that in my mind, but I feel differently. I got compliments from others, teachers and friends. But there's a difference. There's a hundred people who gave me compliments. And there's one person, and she's my mom, and she never gave me compliments. I hear compliments from a hundred people, but I feel my mom's compliment more. Do you understand?"

Our interview had ended. I had switched off the tape recorder and begun gathering my belongings into my bag when Lucy leaned across the table and whispered, "Can I tell you something?"

I nodded.

"I thought about committing suicide."

I put my bag down, surprised. She rushed on to explain herself, her face strangely blank and intent. Now I realized why Lucy was so eager to see me. Another chamber inside her had opened, and let out a bit more of the pressure.

Here in the United States, Asian students such as Lucy have become the model minorities, held up as sterling examples of immigrant perseverance and achievement. But there is another side to this story, which Lucy, a star student, wanted to show me: the cost of so much expectation was very high. It came with a lot of pain and difficulty.

"I have a lot of conflicts in my mind. I want to escape from every single thing. Escape is the easiest way. I know the easiest way is not the best way. I want to get out of this world. I want to disappear. I don't want to care about my family, and I don't want to care about anything else. I want to relax. I want to take a rest."

"How long were you feeling this way?"

"One and a half years. For a long time. It was so hard. My schoolwork was the only thing to forget feelings. I feel so depressed, having this feeling, I try to study so hard, I concentrate to forget it.

"One day I said, 'Mom, I thought about suicide.' And she said, 'That's not good for you.' She was right. It's not a good thing. Sometimes I don't understand myself. I want something so badly, but I couldn't. For example, I try to cut class. But I couldn't. Everybody laugh at me. It's my shame. My friends, everybody else could do it. I can't. And I knew that when I thought about the suicide, I knew I couldn't."

"What made it go away?"

"First of all, my religion. When I have a hard time, I pray to God. I think, My God prevent me to do bad things. Secondly, my mom, I feel sympathy to her. Her life, it's really so sad. Even though my mother was really smart, she couldn't have an opportunity to get higher education. She push me to get more. Since I was young, I have seen that. For a long time. I feel responsible for that. I thought, like, I should be a great daughter for her. Only for her."

Lucy's grandfather had appeared to her in a dream, and that changed her life. Now it was her mother who loomed, and saved her from dangerous and despairing thoughts. Her mother was there, in every snapshot, reminding her that more than one life was tangled into Lucy's; more than one person was depending on her to take her family into the future. Lucy knew this. Once again, she had handed the bouquet of flowers back to her mother, and promised never to forget the woman who had made her who she is.

Marina

ALBANIAN FROM YUGOSLAVIA

Sixteen years old

In my country they don't go to school. My father has never been to school. He works in buildings fixing pipes, boilers. My mother had only four years of education. All she does is clean houses. Most Albanian women clean houses.

All the girls where I come from, everybody goes to church, because that's where the young guys and young girls see each other. Then the guy comes to the father, and he is told to come back in two, three weeks. This is a proposal for marriage.

If I'd stayed in the Bronx with other Yugoslavians, today I would be married. I probably would not be in school. I've turned more Americanized since I moved to Queens. My parents, they've gotten more Americanized too. They realized they would like me to marry an Albanian or Yugoslavian, but they don't want me to marry him that way.

I don't like it in the church in the Bronx. You have to maintain a certain posture. You can't smile too much. You can't look back. They're gossips. I hate that feeling when I'm around those people. My mother doesn't like it when I say that. She says, These are your people, your family. But I can't feel that way in front of them.

I have no Albanian or Yugoslavian friends. All they do is sit around the house and learn how to cook and clean. I want to go to school. I want to say I've done something with my life. I do not want to end up cleaning houses like my mother. I want to have a job that I can be proud of. My mother even says it: God forbid you end up with the job that I have.

Oh my God, my American friends, their family life is so different! They can talk back to their families. I think that's so wrong. Since I was brought up with such respect, I will never ever in my life disrespect my father or my mother. My brothers, as American as they are, they can't do that. If you don't have respect for your parents, then who do you have respect for?

Yulia

Eighteen years old

"I want to be free and not be marrying."

For Yulia, coming to the United States meant joining the land of teenagers, while also discovering the tragedies of adult life. It meant exploring a California dreamland of perfect blue skies, amusement parks, beaches, and waking up to sobering losses of adulthood. In immigration, Yulia has gained a few more years of carefree adolescence, and lost a cherished part of her childhood.

The American idea of teenage—that in-between time when you sort out who you are, experiment, date different people—is unheard of in countries such as Russia. Life has a very clear track: After a person graduates from high school, he or she becomes a grown-up, a parent, a worker. There isn't time or money to try out different identities. If Yulia were living in Russia today, she'd probably be married and starting her own family.

When I first met Yulia and some of her Russian girl-friends at school, I noticed that by American standards they dressed in a very adult way. They all wore tall platform shoes and tight skirts or flared pants, and carried themselves with an air of sophistication. Yulia was a little different. Slender, with light-brown hair and large eyes, she could be a model, yet she was almost unaware of her good looks. Her soft

Yulia

voice trembled with emotion. She seemed more uncertain than the others, as if testing out her grown-up-ness.

Born in a region that was once part of Romania, Yulia grew up in what was considered a "mixed" family: her father was Jewish and her mother was Romanian. Life in Russia was hard, but very stable. She lived in the same house her whole childhood, her father had a good job as an engineer, and her mother was a sales manager. She has two brothers, one a twin and the other a few years older.

Though Yulia's parents were better off than many Russians, they decided to immigrate to the United States for their children's future, and to join her parental grandparents, who had settled in Los Angeles five years earlier. The life that greeted them was much rougher than expected. Yulia's father, who once enjoyed a solid reputation as a professional, now worked for a Russian construction firm, which didn't even pay him a minimum wage. His English was very poor. The apartment they lived in was too small.

Everything Yulia once took for granted—friends, how to act in school, teachers' expectations—reshuffled. Home life was turned topsy-turvy too. Her parents, whom she once looked up to, suddenly became fumbling and shy immigrants. She, on the other hand, was speeding ahead, learning English, picking up all the cues of American culture. Suddenly she was a half grown-up in the household, and her parents depended on her. As was the case for many of the immigrant teenagers I've talked to, these kinds of changes have given Yulia tremendous depth and humanity. "My mom says, 'When you were little, you were behind my back. Now I am behind your back.' "

Then, within a short time of Yulia's family's arrival in Los Angeles, her grandmother died. Her grandfather died soon after. Grief-stricken, Yulia's father tried to press on. But Yulia could tell that life in America was eating him up.

"He was a good person and high-level there," she said. "Now he was at the bottom. It shamed him in front of my mother and in front of us. He thought he would give a good step for us—a car, new clothing, a new room. I was dreaming of my own room and we couldn't afford it, so he was ashamed."

I could hear the empathy that cracked in Yulia's voice. She wanted to communicate how this lovely man came here, sacrificed everything for his children, even his self-esteem. Though Yulia's father didn't talk about his feelings very much, she could sense his suffering. "It's hard, because here is not so good for my parents," she went on. "I see this and I can understand this from what's happening. They know they have to go through this just for us."

While Yulia was trying to provide some comfort to her displaced father, she found another mentor who helped her find her own footing in America. The day she and her family arrived at the airport, she had met a young man, a friend of her cousin's who was four years older than she. For their first date, he took her to a beautiful spot by the ocean. Then they began to date seriously. Soon Yulia was part of an octet: four Russian girls and four Russian boys would pile into their cars and explore the California landscape of miniature golf, movies, the San Diego Zoo.

Yulia's boyfriend, who had been in the States for five years and worked for a television production company to support his mother and grandparents, provided what her own father could not: confidence, a sense of ease about this new culture. He prodded the shy Yulia to speak up in stores or in class, and gave her lectures on self-reliance.

"He taught me a lot of things about America and about this lifestyle. He taught me about people respecting me. I was very shy and he said, 'You have to talk very loud so that people hear you.' He was talking about self-respect, because in Russia they don't teach us about our self-respect. Here, if you don't respect yourself, other people won't respect you.

"From the first day you have to show that you're not a weak person. If you show you're a weak person, they will treat you like a weak person. To get a job, for example, I was afraid of the interview, I was afraid I do not speak English well. He say, 'You're a beautiful girl, you don't have to be ashamed of this. You don't have to be afraid. Everything for you is here.' "

While her boyfriend boosted her self-confidence, and egged her to try American-style freedom, Yulia's parents tried to keep her at home, close to them. At first her mother objected to her boyfriend because he wasn't attending college. And dating, this mix between independence and dependence, being in and out of the home, was strange to a Russian family. They were especially protective of Yulia, since she is a girl.

"They treat me differently than my brothers," she explained. "If my brothers are going out, they don't say where they're going, with whom they're going, when they're coming back. 'Father, why is brother going wherever they want?' I ask. 'You treat me unfairly and I want to go out too.' And he says, 'That's because I love you too much.' He's scared. Because I'm a girl, they hold me."

One evening, while Yulia's parents were attending English class, her father's face turned ashen-gray. His words became garbled. He excused himself from the classroom and went into the corridor. Finally, somebody called an ambulance, but by the time he reached the hospital, he'd suffered a stroke. The stress, Yulia explained, had been too much to bear.

Hopeful that he would recover, the family kept a vigil at the hospital. Her father was alert and would joke with Yulia about her boyfriend. But ten days later he suffered another stroke and died. The family had been in the country five months.

A few days after our first interview, I visited Yulia at her home in West Hollywood. She lives on a pretty, tree-lined street where people walk by and call to each other in Russian. Late-afternoon sun slanted across the palm trees and splashed the chalky walls of the apartment building. Inside the immaculate apartment, Yulia was watching the beginning of the Academy Awards show with another Russian girl. Avid star-watchers, the two girls commented on the different gowns and told me they have seen *Titanic* several times.

Excitedly Yulia gave me a tour of her home, which consisted of a living room, a dining area, and two bedrooms—one for her mother, the other for her two brothers. Yulia used to share a bedroom with her brothers, and though she now sleeps in the living room, she pointed to the bedroom wall that was once filled with her stuffed animals. It reminded me that Yulia was still a young girl, who also has the gravity and intensity of an adult.

As we sat around the table, the conversation turned easily to her father. I could see that Yulia really wanted to talk about him. Her pale, oval face shone. She brought out a photo album and showed me pictures from Russia and the United States, pointing out her father, a slight, blond-haired man who barely looked his forty-three years when he died. There were also pictures of Yulia vacationing with her boyfriend, the two of them astride a Jet Ski, or dressed up with friends at a restaurant. But it was her father who was released into the quiet, dusk-filled room, like a genie from a bottle, wisping around us, both heavily present and painfully absent.

"We were like best friends," she told me. "I was more with my father and I was his favorite. He loves all three of us but I would talk to him more. He worked until twelve at night, so I would wait for him and we'd talk together. I liked to talk to him. He knew everything in my life. Once I went to the camp and I came back; he said, 'Julie, did you try smoking?' I said, 'No.' He said, 'Look at me, did you try smoking?' I said, 'Yeah.' He said, 'Why you lying at me?' " She laughs, as if caught in her deceit. "He knew everything about me."

She described the months after her father's death, how she would come home and find her mother cocooned in her room, depressed. "It was very, very, very hard for her to be alone. That was hard for us too. I won't let her stay alone. That makes me stay home every time. She was very depressed. Everything was so sad every time. Everything was dark, no music, no TV. I didn't want to come home for a while."

More and more responsibilities fell on Yulia. Not only did she have to keep up her mother's spirits, but she was responsible for translating the bills into Russian and conducting business. Her mother went to look for better work, and Yulia always accompanied her to interviews. Then, Yulia and her mother began to clash. While Yulia's boyfriend gave her a taste of American-style independence, her mother, particularly in a time of grief, wanted to enforce some old-fashioned strictness. But Yulia had already tasted her freedom, and she didn't want to give it up.

Yulia is in a confusing, in-between space. In Russia she was a child, protected by her parents. In the States a whole new phase stretches before her, that of playful teenage life. At the same time, since her father's death, she has also become more of an adult, helping her mother cope. Indeed, Yulia and her mother are battling about the very meaning of being eighteen. In Russia, turning eighteen meant suddenly becoming a grown-up. Here in the States, it means exploration and freedom, remaining carefree without too many adult worries weighing her down.

"I have a lot of arguments with my mom. I never had arguments with my mom in Russia. I didn't go out, didn't have that many friends. And here on the weekends I want to go out. She's going, 'What is it, a holiday? Why do you have to go out?' I'm eighteen years old and I have more freedom now. And she's like, 'You're eighteen years old,' and doesn't mean anything to her. And for me, it means a lot."

Yulia misses her father, and how these conflicts could have been sorted out through talk. With him, she could test out her grown-up-ness, because he treated her as a person with opinions and a point of view. "These fights I have with my mom are all because she doesn't want to talk to me. She knows that she's right and she thinks that I'm a child, and she doesn't give me the freedom to speak. If we are more like adults, we don't have problems."

To add to the confusion, recently Yulia and her boyfriend broke up because they often fought about what she calls "adult" problems. Yulia wanted him to go to college and was jealous when he spent time with another girl. He felt she was too dependent on him. "From the beginning I was dependent on my parents," she said. "And then I was dependent on him. And then I was like a little child. He said, If you're dependent on someone, then it's no good. You have to be on your own, so make your life what you want it to be."

On Valentine's Day, he suggested they be friends. "A serious relationship at my age is too hard," she explained. "When you have a serious relationship with a guy, you have serious problems. It's like you're adult, and I don't want to be adult. I'm eighteen now, I want to enjoy my young years."

As if convincing herself that it's the right thing to do, several times she remarked: "It's better for us to be friends. Because we're young, and a serious relationship is not good for us because we have more to learn."

Since the breakup, her fights with her mother have escalated. It was one thing for Yulia to go out chaperoned by her older boyfriend. It's another when she wants to get in a car with her Russian girlfriends and have fun. This is something her mother cannot fathom: a girl alone, relishing her independence. Her mother, Yulia claims, keeps looking back at her own experience, how at eighteen she had already moved out and worked on her own. "She treats me like a child," Yulia repeated.

In one way, Yulia finds teenage life easier in America. It's about discovering herself, being independent. In another, more subtle way, it's harder. There are no clear rules about relationships, or how to balance home life and friends. Yulia, who keeps in touch with her girlfriends in Russia, recently learned that one friend is getting married. The news shocked her, even though she knows it's normal back there. Her own life is so different: she's broken up a romance after two years, is casting about for her own form of independence, and squabbles with her mother over who she is. She's torn between the different poles of her life: her peers, who tell her not to settle down, versus her mother, who urges her to stay home, cook, and take care of the family. Yulia keeps trying to grasp that more ambiguous goal: to resist being defined by family or by marriage; to live, for a while, in her own in-between space.

"If I get married with a guy that means I'm free," she explained. "If I'm not married, I'm not free. I want to be free and not be marrying."

It is a sign of Yulia's deepening maturity that she doesn't entirely blame her mother. She is able to take a step back, and see her own struggles as part of a bigger conflict between parent and child. "I think this period will pass. I think this has to happen in every family. There's an expression in Russian: 'When your child grows up, you understand you are old.' "

When our conversation turned to Yulia's future, she offered a remarkable plan that seemed to resolve all these conflicts: she and her family want to buy a house and open a school together. Her dream is to become a child psychologist—from her babysitting and camp-counselor jobs, she's observed that young children often need an outsider to help with their problems. Her mother, who is now enrolled in a physician's-assistant program, will get her degree, and her older brother is helping to earn money to save for a car and a house. Her mother also has a new boyfriend, who will join them.

"We have a big, big, big plan for our family. We want to open a kindergarten like a business. My mom likes kids and I like kids. We do everything for this. There are five of us in the family. All of us are big, and we can work all together. There's no children anymore. We can help each other."

And so Yulia has created her own vision of in-betweenness. She has harnessed some of the practical, go-getter quality she learned from her assimilated boyfriend to an immigrant's powerful sense of sharing with the family. "I'm in a situation where I have to do something to have a better life," she explained. The blow of Yulia's father's death brought this family closer together, and made them realize how much they must lean on one other. Yulia has found a way to make sense of her conflicting impulses: to be free and stay attached, to belong to the world she knows, while staking a claim in this strange new landscape.

Veronica

Eighteen years old

EL SALVADOR

I grew up in San Salvador, the capital of El Salvador. My aunt owned a bakery and I used to work delivering the bread. My mother and stepfather was already here.

I did not want to leave, because I never lived with my mother. I always live with my aunts, my cousins. When my mom told me I was going to come to Los Angeles, I felt like saying no. I didn't understand my feelings. I knew my aunt better than my mother.

I came here on July 25, at twelve o'clock, in 1992. I was eleven years old and came with my aunts, right to Los Angeles. Now I live in South Central Los Angeles and I have a little brother, almost three years old, born here. In my neighborhood, there are not many people from El Salvador. There are not many teenagers.

My mother never told me how was Los Angeles. I feel a lot of fears. I didn't know the people, the place; I feel strange. So, for the first month, I didn't want to go out, I want to stay in the home all the time.

Here I have to stay inside, take care of my little brother, do everything in the house, cook, clean the house, make the beds, everything. So it's difficult.

I have friends in school, but they live very far away. We talk about boys. Boys, classes, and grades. We talk to the boys but we are not allowed to go out with them. My mother says I have to study first. Sometimes I disagree.

Nine months ago, I met a boy. He was working in the market we go to on Saturday. Sometimes he came to school, lunchtime. He was from El Salvador, and he would visit me, but we couldn't go places.

I feel love for this boy. It was love, I think. I was thinking about him all the time. I was calling to the work, wanting to know what he's doing, everything. Then he has some problems. He has to go back to El Salvador.

So, every night, I write a letter for him, saying goodbye. I never sent him the letters, so I kept all the letters. One day, it was the last letter I was writing to him, I was in my room. I was writing the letter, my father opened the door. What are you doing? he say. Nothing, I say, very scared. I want to see what you're hiding over there. He read the letters and everything.

That night, we start to fight. I go to sleep at like two o'clock, so my mother came home and she pick me up and start to fight and hit me. My stepfather said I was a bitch because I wanted to be with a man. He never understands. He said that my grades were down, that was the big problem. Like F and E. I say, Okay, I understand you, but I feel sometimes lonely. I'm alone all the time. My parents are still angry with me. Now I feel nothing. Sometimes I feel sad. But I don't feel love for the boy now. My mother, she says this is the way it has to be.

Sorianyi

Eighteen years old

"I'm used to being alone my whole life."

Sorianyi is a survivor. She is a young woman who was born out of survival: her mother gave birth to her when she was running from the Khmer Rouge* at the end of the war in Cambodia. She is a daughter who has survived being abandoned by her father, a girl who has survived homelessness, an immigrant who is determined to survive the tough streets of Los Angeles. And she is a survivor who lives for another survivor: her beloved mother.

"I just think about my future and my school," she told me several times, repeating it like a chant. It is as if, when her mother was running from the brutal soldiers who wanted to kill her, Sorianyi absorbed a survivor's instinct for self-preservation, a clear vision of the road ahead. Despite many setbacks since she came to the States, she is remarkably cheerful and focused. Nothing—not the difficulties of a new language, bad living situations, a father's callousness—will keep her from finding her way in her new country.

---

* The Khmer Rouge was a communist revolutionary group that became genocidal in its efforts to purge the country of "class enemies," such as anybody who wore glasses. They were responsible for the deaths of two million Cambodians. They were eventually driven out by the Vietnamese. Their leader, Pol Pot, died only recently.

Sorianyi

I met Sorianyi on a warm spring afternoon at a brand-new elementary school not far from Belmont High School in Los Angeles, where she is a student. Sorianyi works here as a teacher's assistant every afternoon—it is part of a very full schedule that includes classes, special programs, housework at the shelter where she lives, plus a job on evenings and weekends. Sorianyi told me she likes all this activity. "I like to be busy. I like to be free."

Sorianyi has a round, open face and smiles easily. She wore her long hair clipped back neatly with a barrette and was dressed in jeans, blazer, and crisp white shirt. She was eager to tell her story, and spoke at a very rapid pace. At the end of the war in Cambodia, she told me, her parents were fleeing their village, trying to get across the border to refugee camps in Thailand. But Sorianyi's mother was pregnant and could not run anymore. Her parents agreed that her father would go ahead to the camps and on to the United States, and would then send for his wife. Only that never happened.

"My dad told her that he's going to come back and bring her here. He never did that. He forgot his word."

After Sorianyi was born, her mother opened a tailoring shop in a small town to support her daughter; when Sorianyi started junior high, they moved to the capital city of Phnom Penh. Sorianyi grew up knowing very little of her father. Sometimes he would write to them and send a little money, but years could pass before they would hear from him. Devoted to her mother, Sorianyi grew used to the long hours of solitude and studying. She didn't miss a larger family, brothers and sisters, or a father. "In our family there were only two people all the time."

As Sorianyi grew older, there were hints that her father might not have told them the complete truth about his life in the United States. Once she and her mother were visiting relatives of Sorianyi's father when they saw photos of another woman and children in America. Clearly, he had remarried and started another family. Still Sorianyi's mother wrote to her husband to ask him to send for her daughter, so that Sorianyi could finish high school and go to college in the States. College in Cambodia required too much money—money Sorianyi's mother didn't have.

At seventeen, Sorianyi got into her first airplane and flew across the ocean to live with a man she'd never met, and to be part of a family she had just found out about. But there were more surprises ahead.

When Sorianyi arrived in Los Angeles, she discovered that her father didn't even live with his second wife and children. Two years before, because of "some problems," he'd become a monk, and lived in a Buddhist temple, where no women were allowed. Her father did not send for Sorianyi because he wanted to help her. He sent for her to help him, now that he was without his children and wife.

"He thought that he's old and he has nobody to take care of him. That's why he brought me here."

For the first three months, Sorianyi couldn't go to school. She went to the temple every day to help her father. To make matters worse, the living situation her father had set up quickly soured. First her father had arranged for Sorianyi to board with a Chinese family. Sorianyi isn't sure what happened, but she believes her father didn't pay them the money he had promised. She was sent to live with a Cambodian family, who expected that she would do housework in exchange for room and board. Sorianyi was miserable. "I cannot study and I like to be alone. I could not be alone."

Fortunately, Sorianyi had the good sense to speak to a teacher, who found a shelter for girls who are in trouble. It is far from perfect: The shelter is in a rough part of town, and she never goes out at night. Sorianyi, who desperately wants privacy and solitude, must share a room with three other girls, and they cannot come back to the shelter during the day. Because the shelter is for girls who have gotten into trouble, Sorianyi keeps to herself, for she fears the other girls will influence her. "I feel like if I have a girlfriend I'm going to turn bad."

Still, Sorianyi has made the best of it. She likes how everyone pitches in at the shelter. She attended a program at school that showed her how to get a job and recently landed a position at Hardee's. And she and the psychology teacher are already working on getting her into a better shelter program, one that provides apartments for girls who do well in school. Sorianyi hopes that in a few months she'll move into an apartment with another girl and will be able to come and go as she pleases.

"When I live in the shelter, we have structure and they help us. You have to do it together. They have a cook, we just clean our rooms. Everybody does the same. In Cambodian family I have to do housework. In the shelter I don't have to live under someone. I feel I have more freedom."

Sorianyi has coped by plunging fully into her new life— school, part-time jobs, programs. She stays busy, because in busyness she can find herself. It's this very independence and clarity of purpose that anger her father, who assumed his long-lost daughter was coming to the United States in order to tend to him dutifully. He continues to live at the temple and is bitter that his daughter does not come and visit him more often and help out.

"To be honest, me and my father, we don't get along," she told me. "I don't understand him. When I stay with him I feel bad, my feeling is not happy. When I go to the temple he wants me to do this, do that. Sometimes I tell him I have homework and I cannot go. He gets angry. Now he stays angry with me. He blame me a lot."

"About what?"

"Sometimes I have a little mistake and he make my mistake go big. Like sometimes I don't call him. When I call him, he told me, If I'm busy don't call him. He doesn't understand. I'm tired from school and I'm so very busy. I think, 'Why doesn't he let me have a little time to relax?' "

Sorianyi seems resigned to, yet irritated by, these clashes with her father. The only moments of pain she could speak of are times when she's observed her father with his other children. "Sometimes I feel jealous when I see he care more about his other children. He call them, talk to them very good. He talk to me rude."

Sorianyi's fights with her father could be a struggle between any father and daughter: he wants her to stay in more, help him out; she wants her independence. The difference here is that Sorianyi's father is a stranger to her, and she never forgets it. She harbors no illusions about family loyalty; she sees her father purely as a means to reach a successful and secure life in the United States. It's this unsparing, clear vision that keeps her on track. "He never gave my mom a lot of money to take care of me. He just bring me from Cambodia to here. That's the big thing he did."

Sorianyi is completely loyal to her mother. Every class she takes, every hour she spends studying or working at the fast-food restaurant, every scary walk through the dark Los Angeles streets, is done for her mother. Her mother carried her through dangerous times, then scrimped, saved, and worked. Now Sorianyi is doing the same for her. She will carry her mother into the future; she will eventually be the parent to her own parent. "I care only about my mom," she told me. "About him, whatever he does, that's his story. My mom, she takes care of me a lot. She lets me go to school, she wants me to be a good person. I don't think about him. I just think about my future and my school."

So strong is Sorianyi's resolve to take care of herself, to be independent, that she's told her mother nothing of her problems in housing. Sorianyi's mother does not have a phone, so Sorianyi writes to her, telling her only cheerful news. "I didn't want her to worry about me. Right now I tell her everything is okay, take care of herself, not to be sick. When I bring her here, I will tell her everything. She is alone, I don't want her to be lonely."

"You're not going to tell her that you live in the shelter?"

"No, I'm not. Because if I tell her she's going to be really worried and upset. She's old, she's not in good health, and she's very thin. If she thinks a lot, it's going to make her sick. Nobody cares for her, because nobody stays with her."

Another teenager might have crumpled under the pressures and disappointments that Sorianyi has faced. She came to a strange country, all by herself, and found herself again and again in situations that exploited her: families who made her work, a father who treated her like a servant. But Sorianyi has a deep core of resourcefulness. As the only child of a woman who is herself a war survivor, Sorianyi has formed powerful habits of self-reliance. The isolation that might be unbearable for others is not a hardship for her, simply because she likes her own company. "In Cambodia, I sit in the room alone and study. I stay alone. I didn't get involved. Also, I never lived in a big family. I'm used to being alone all my life." Even with her best friend, an Indian girl with whom she shares talk about classes and future plans, Sorianyi keeps at a distance. "Sometimes with my best friend I feel she bothers me. I don't want to talk. I want to walk alone and be quiet. To be independent."

At the end of the interview, Sorianyi peppered me with questions about my work. When she heard I had a gradu-ate degree, she asked if she could get a better job that way. Her biggest concern was how to establish herself so she could bring her mother over. Her sense of focus was breathtaking. "Right now I work and go to college and get a job. Because they say when I am American citizen I can bring my mother here. So now I try my best."

This is how Sorianyi holds herself together. This prom-ise is the opening at the end of the long road. It gets her through the ups and downs of her arrival, the shuttle between strange homes, the fights with her father. Sorianyi belongs to no one but her mother. She keeps herself busy, always thinking of that thin woman, miles and miles away, bent over a sewing machine. And I knew, as we said good-bye outside the school, that Sorianyi will again survive.

One year after I met Sorianyi, she was elected president of the student body at Belmont High School.

Claris

Claris

Sixteen years old

"I have a tree in my heart."

To know Claris, you need to know all the people that make up who she is. Claris grew up in a town in the Dominican Republic where all the neighbors had known her since she was a little girl. The local shopkeepers let customers pay at the end of the month, and her grandparents kept a close and strict watch on Claris and her sister. Coming to the United States, Claris had to learn a whole new meaning for community. "In my country, if something happens to you, the neighbors care for you," Claris explained. "Here hardly anybody say hello. It's like you don't have nobody."

I first noticed Claris in an advanced ESL class at Flushing High School, where a story, "The Enormous Wings," by Gabriel García Márquez, was being discussed. Claris sat in the second row and kept raising her hand, gladly piping up to explain what magic realism meant to her. She described her experiences with spirits, and how her grandfather in the Dominican Republic wanted to be buried in a box underneath their house. Claris has a childlike, fantastic imagination, and her English trips off her tongue in an eager rush.

When we talked later, I saw there was something truly sweet and protected about Claris. Her eyes shone with a rare innocence; she was not far from the dreamy play-world of girlhood. In some ways, this is Claris's asset—she is very calm and trusting. She also seemed vague about her future. She was so surrounded by a familiar and loving world, the future in America seemed hazy and far away.

Claris's mother had originally studied to be an accountant, but she left the Dominican Republic because of problems with her husband's family. Once here she was only able to find work in a factory. For several years, Claris and her older sister were raised by their maternal grandparents; when she was eleven years old and her sister was thirteen, they came to the United States. Claris recalls what it was like when she first arrived: "Now, in my country, when you live in a house, it's a *whole* house. So, when I saw the house in Corona, I thought, 'Oh my god.' I say, 'I live in the attic, the attic is mine!' And my sister was like, 'The second floor is mine, then!'

"Then the owner of the house came out and said, 'You live on the second floor.'

"I'm like, okay. I think, 'I'll sleep next to the window.' But when we get into the second floor, we saw it was divided by two! One is a studio, the other is more like an apartment. We had the studio. I get in there, saw the doors from the closet, and thought, 'Is that the bedroom? It's so small!' Then I saw another door; that was the bathroom. 'Hey, small house,' I thought. I like it anyway."

A few weeks later, she and her sister were alone for the first time in their new apartment. They heard a strange hissing noise in the walls. Frightened, they went and knocked on the next-door neighbor's door. "I thought maybe explosion was going to happen. I went next door with my sister. 'Can you come over, because something is happening, some kind of sound?' we ask the lady. She come over and she start laughing. 'Don't you worry, that's not going to hurt you. It's just the heat coming on.' And she left."

Not only did the houses seem small and the community large and impersonal, but Claris found American kids too mature for their age, too wild and dangerous. "The kids here, it's like they're not kids. Because they prefer to cut. Already in third, fourth grade, they're thinking about girl-friends, boyfriends. They like to play with violence." She laughed. "Where I come from, we play with dolls. We used to talk about the teachers."

"What do kids talk about here?"

"Sex, drugs. How they goin' to kill somebody. A lot of violence. They think like old people. They want to get attention from people, but they don't know how. Person-ally, I think they should go to school."

"Do you feel pressure?"

"Sometimes. Sometimes they don't believe that I'm the way I am. They think I'm a little girl, like a mommy's girl. They like to smoke. I don't feel the fun.

"In my country, girlfriends warn me, they tell me, 'If you do something really wrong, you disappoint me a lot.' Every-where I go in my country, everyone live that way. The neigh-bors, the kids. And within myself it makes sense. Why you going to do something wrong, when you know its conse-quences? If you give yourself self-respect, everybody respects you. Not only to yourself, to your body too. These girls are out of control. I'm not saying girls from my country are per-fect, but in my country it's a shame for the whole family.

"Most of my closest friends are Dominican. I have same beliefs as they have. Kind of old-style. Like, you have to wait until you get married. Go to school. When you do something really wrong, you should talk to somebody. If you can't talk to your mother, talk to your best friend."

"Have you seen any of your friends get in trouble?"

"My best friend, she started to cut school, started to get into drugs, into gangs, she get out of control. Her mother wasn't paying attention to her anymore. So I made a law. Nobody talked to her, nobody looked at her. She couldn't deal with it. Now she's back to school, she gets good grades. She came back."

This is Claris's favorite theme: the web of family, friends, and neighborhood that surround and nourish her. Even though Claris and her sister and mother have moved to Astoria, which is considered a slightly better neighborhood, she considers Corona, where the Dominicans live, her real home. Every day after school, she and her sister go there until her mother picks them up and they continue home. Claris loves how the shopkeepers know their customers and forgive them if they don't have enough money, keeping a little notebook of accounts.

"It's kind of weird," she says of her new home. "Astoria is more safe than Corona. But I know Corona, I know what's dangerous. I know the bad and the good people."

I got some glimpse into this on a day I spent with Claris, her sister, and their friends. Every afternoon, the four girls meet outside school, kiss one another on the cheek, and slowly walk to the subway, sometimes accompanied by a boy. They take the Number 7, an elevated train that shuttles past Shea Stadium, the old World's Fair grounds, its silvery Unisphere glinting in the distance. Down below, in the streets of brick semidetached homes and apartment houses, lies one immigrant neighborhood after another: Colombian, Dominican, Indian, Greek. The girls get off a few stops later on Roosevelt Avenue, a busy thoroughfare, and take a leisurely circuit of the neighborhood. Corona is like a chunk of the Dominican Republic sitting under the slatted shadows of the elevated tracks.

First we ran into a former teacher on our way to a sneaker shop run by a friend of theirs, where they talked about Selena. All of them loved Selena, the Mexican-American singer who was killed by a crazed fan. "She's so normal," Claris explained. "She's an actress, famous. But she always was for her people. She's one of us. Born here, but she felt as if she's born in Mexico. She kept her values."

Next we made our way to the bakery, where a relative who worked behind the counter greeted them. Then we walked down the block, waving to various people, a dance teacher, another relative. For a short while we sat on the steps of the church where Claris had her confirmation. On the curb in front of us a man fixed a car—he was a friend of her uncle's.

Though these streets are Claris's home, the community that protects her, they can also turn dangerous. A year ago, she lost her beloved uncle in a robbery. He represented much of what Claris values: he was constantly circulating around the neighborhood, visiting people. "He was a typical Dominican guy. All over the place. Even if he needs money, he give it to you, he doesn't care if you pay him back. He gave advice to everybody. He was the middle one, who tried to connect."

She recalled how, the week before he died, her uncle urged Claris to get along better with her sister. And the day he died, he made a special point of giving Claris's mother his umbrella because it was raining. It was this trait of helping out that brought him to a fatal end.

On that gray, drizzly day, while her uncle stopped by a friend's grocery store, a young boy rushed in to rob the store. Ironically, the boy was the shopkeeper's nephew.

Claris's uncle stepped in, and tried to calm the situation down. He knew the boy was desperate and poor, but he pleaded with him to remember this was a relative. When that didn't work, the uncle, trained as a boxer, tried to wrestle the boy down. The nephew had a gun, and shot Claris's uncle dead.

The shock of his death hit Claris's family hard. When the body was brought back to the Dominican Republic, Claris could not bear to go for the burial. To her, her cherished island is now associated with death. Her sister fell into a deep depression, from which she still hasn't completely recovered. And Claris keeps running over the last times she spoke to her uncle. She dreams of him constantly, and can't forget how she meant to ask him to be her godfather for her confirmation but never found the time. By the church, she points to the funeral home where everyone came to pay respects.

Our last stop was Claris's friend's house, where the girls usually end up and like to fry plantains and sometimes dance to merengue, a rhythmic dance music popular in the Dominican Republic. They stay in the kitchen, sprawled on a small couch and a few chairs. A Dominican boy came by on his way back from baseball practice and stayed a little while, then left. It seemed part of their afternoon ritual, comforting and familiar.

"The problem with Dominican boys," she told me later, "is they're too possessive. Too macho. You go to a party and they don't want you to dance with anyone else. Puerto Rican boys are not so bad. They accept American culture more. They're more free. They're a mix."

When I asked her if she missed her father, her eyes shone once more and she grew reflective.

"I would say I miss him but I got people in levels. I have a tree in my heart. My father is one of these branches—

he's special when he's there, when he makes me feel that he's there for me. But he thinks like a little kid. He doesn't use his mind like a grown-up person. I love him so much, but not as much as my mother, because she's really been there for me."

At the end of the day, Claris walked me to the subway and we talked again about her life. This time, some of her sunniness was clouded with other fears. Though she feels loved and protected in her community, she is also aware of the coldness of American society, out there. "In this country, you're alone," she said. "My mother faces discrimination, but she doesn't like to talk about it."

At school, though she hasn't been singled out for discrimination, she's felt the hostility directed at Hispanics in general, the stereotyping by teachers. "You feel humiliated, left out. I feel it's my fault and cry and get depressed. There was a teacher in my class, with five Hispanic kids, the others Asians and Indians. The Pakistani and Indian and Hispanic kids didn't pass. They say, The Asian kids are smart, all of you dumb. They always criticize the way we talk. It's true, the Asian kids work hard and want to succeed. But not all."

Claris admitted she wanted her life to stay the same in this small wedge of the Dominican Republic here in New York City. "I'm afraid of college, to be apart, new things. When I go to college, I want to stay at home. I don't like changes. Everything on your own, the classes big. Maybe I won't be accepted. I'm kind of afraid."

Two years later, I learned that Claris had managed to bridge the distance between home, community, and her future. She was attending Hunter College in Manhattan, a competitive city college a subway ride away.

"Caroline"

HAITI

Eighteen years old

I grew up with my grandmother, on my father's side. My father brought me to Miami when I was nine. I don't remember much about Haiti. I just know that my parents weren't there to raise me. I've been raising myself since I was nine.

When I used to live in Miami, most of the people who took me in—it was more to take care of children and cook and clean. I moved to [Brooklyn in] New York City with a distant cousin; I call her my aunt. She took me in for the same reason, to help with her daughter.

I know in the Caribbeans you get really bad beatings, but to the point where you get flinged around, thrown across the floor, and kicked and everything. Oh my gosh, when I saw her beating her daughter, I tried to stop her. She told me to just get out of here, it's not my business. But after a while it did become my business because she started hitting me. And I was basically abused from the time I was thirteen to sixteen.

Every week we had to buy, like, three, four mops because she would break it on us. It was kinda hard. One time she had beaten me and then that was the first time she shed my blood. She hit me with a blender, on my eye. Blood started coming down, but I didn't feel anything at the moment. 'Cause I was shocked. That never happened before.

It went on for three years straight. I felt hurt. My grandmother used to say, "Never disobey or disrespect an adult." I didn't feel like anybody cared for me, because all my life I had to do that for myself. After a while I didn't even want to face my report card. I would not stay in school. Because the only freedom I had was getting out of school and being outside.

One night I'm at my friend's and I'm like, "You know what? I'm not going home. I don't care." My friend called the house.

My aunt was like, "If you don't come home, then don't come home at all." I went home the next day and I found all my things packed up. But she would not let me go for a whole two weeks. Then I was putting my things in my closet and she was really acting up. I just looked at her, and I was like, "Go ahead. Just hit me. That'll give me a better reason to find somewhere to stay if you hit me." She just looked at me and put the broom back. That night I left.

Well, I lived in a basement where a guy friend of mine lived. It was scary down there because there was only guys down there. They gave me a room to stay in and I locked it up. I would go to my friends' houses to eat. I was cutting school and everything. I ended up moving in with my friend again and I started studying the Bible in that house. And I became a disciple.

My father never did my immigration papers right. And the law came up. If you don't have your papers you have to go right back home. I was shocked. I had not been home for such a long time. I can't even speak the language properly. I was so scared. I went to The Door; it's a program for teenagers. The lawyer gave me information on how I could get my papers. I had to get everything done before I turned eighteen or they could easily send me back home. I found out foster care would hold me until I'm twenty-one.

Whenever I would call my father he would never be there. I know my father could find me if he wants to. I always leave a track he could follow. I don't know if he's dead or alive. He was a traveler, he used to bring people to the United States illegally. That was his job. So I'm thinking he got busted. I don't know what happened.

Especially around Christmastime, I was just crying. It feels like everybody has their family. My family right now is my church. I love my church so much. When you go to the church, you don't want to leave.

To Be Young, Muslim, and Female in America Today: three stories

To be Muslim in America today is to be marked as different. The most obvious symbol of a Muslim girl is her head covering. There are a number of different names for this garment. A *chador* is the most complete body covering. In Arabic, *hijab* means both "covering the body" and "a modest deportment." In South Asia, *purdah* has a related meaning that also implies secluding women. *Khimar* is an Arabic word for the actual veil or scarf, which would be called a *burqa* in South Asia. Not all Muslim girls wear a head covering, though in traditional Muslim culture, once a girl reaches a certain age, she covers her head as a sign of respect and propriety. In America, this head covering can be a painful mark that sets a girl apart from other young people and makes her a target of cruel remarks.

For girls raised under Muslim laws, the biggest change they encounter is attending school with boys. They can react in different ways: mix easily in coed situations; resist any new contacts; or experiment in risky ways. The following are conversations with three very different Muslim girls—Farida, Nubaisha, and Ashrat—whose reactions to America cover these possibilities.

Farida
Seventeen years old

BANGLADESH

> *"It's more important to sacrifice for the people who love you."*

Talking to Farida showed me the hidden power of the head covering.

Though Farida has weathered some painful shocks in emigrating to the United States, she also seemed more composed than most teenagers. Her whole manner was light and easy, but when I talked to her, I quickly saw how morally serious she is, and how devout. She makes sure, for instance, to pray five times a day. At the same time, she does not wear her faith as a heavy burden. It seems natural, like the dark scarf she wears loosely tied around her head, and which she lets slip to her shoulders when we are alone.

Farida's grace and ease with herself are all the more remarkable because she has a speech impediment. Her words seem to get backed up, and it takes a few seconds for them to come tumbling out. She speaks in plain, simple sentences that are highly revealing and also leave a zone of privacy around herself. Now and then her sly sense of humor also flashes through. Slowly, as we talked, I uncovered the different layers that make up Farida, until she finally revealed the source that gives her so much hope and such clear understanding.

In some ways, Farida was prepared for immigration since she was a little girl in Dhaka, Bangladesh. Her father, who was trained as a civil engineer, often went off to other countries for work. When she was three years old, he went to Oman, and only came back two years later. When she

Farida

was seven, he left for Libya, and once more returned after two years. This time, he stayed at home until Farida was fourteen, and then, one day, announced that the family would move with him to the United States.

Though she'd grown used to her father's absences, Farida did not want to leave. She loved her home in Dhaka: the tin-roofed house that her father had built, the yard and trees, her school and girlfriends. Her uncle lived with them, and there were always relatives in Dhaka. Then, on school holidays, she went to visit her grandparents, aunts and uncles, and cousins in their village. When she and her family said goodbye to their relatives at the airport, Farida said, "I was crying so much, I don't want to go there. It was bad." She added, "It's still bad. I miss the whole thing. My home, my school, everything I still miss, still now."

Immigration was rough on her family. Her mother, used to being surrounded by her brothers and sisters, was terribly lonely. Her father found work as a supervisor in a factory, but "It's okay, not that good. Just okay." Farida's first encounters in school were difficult. "The other people, they laughed at me, in my classes. Because I had my dress on from Bangladesh, they laughed. My English wasn't so good."

A few days later, she persuaded her parents to let her go to school in jeans. Her father agreed, though her mother made Farida promise that she would switch into her Bangladeshi outfit when she came home. Farida felt she needed to blend in with American kids, but the new clothes felt very, very strange. "In my country, boys have a different dress and girls have a different dress. It's the Muslim rule: girls can't follow the guys."

"So how did it feel to change?" I asked.

She burst into laughter; a brightness shone in her eyes. "Like a boy!" She added with amazement, "I realized I was like a guy."

Perhaps most difficult of all is that Farida has yet to make a single Bangladeshi friend in her school. She lives in the College Point neighborhood of Queens, where there are very few other Bangladeshi families. "There's nobody from my country. It feels bad, you know." Sometimes she and her family go to Astoria, where other Bangladeshi families live, or to mosques nearby. Farida has been dismayed by what she's seen.

"People who are from my country, they are not the same. They changed. Now they are talking, they are American now. That feels bad, you know. They don't pray. They don't like the people from their country. They say we are poor, bad, and stupid. I don't like to go there. They changed too much."

To her, American kids show a shocking amount of disrespect—in the classroom, to their parents. "They are more selfish," she explained. "In my country, a girl, if she likes a guy to marry, but their parents say, 'No, you can't do it,' then they don't do it. They sacrifice for them. Here they don't do it."

"To you that's selfish."

"Yeah, for me that's selfish. It's more important to sacrifice for the people who love you."

Very often, when immigrant teenagers are thrust into a vastly different culture, it can create a great deal of internal conflict. They can feel confused and tempted by their new surroundings, or defensive and judgmental. This is especially true for young people raised under traditional Muslim law, which rules much of their daily life and is so different from American teenage culture.

Not so with Farida. She holds to her own beliefs, but does not look down at the other young people. In the hallways, she calls hello to various students, all of them of different backgrounds; at home, she watches American TV shows. To Farida's family, tradition does not mean holding back. They draw strength from both old ways and new achievements. Her own father grew up poor, and worked his way up by means of his own abilities and education. Always, Farida, who hopes one day to become a doctor, has been encouraged in her studies. One of her teachers told me she was a naturally bright student, a beautiful writer.

For Farida, Islam is not just a dogma, but a deep well-spring of faith and strength that allows her to sail through the choppy waters of her arrival. It is a set of values that are instilled day in, day out, prayer after prayer. "It makes me feel more safe," she said of her religion.

For our second interview, Farida and I met in the conference room at Flushing High School in Queens, New York. It is a room that is chock-full of history: there are signed footballs from the twenties, framed scholarship awards, basketball trophies. Farida was fixated on a photograph of the 1955 honor society. Three prim rows of boys and girls, the boys in their bow ties, the girls with their hair neatly rolled, their bobby socks. "It's so different!" she exclaimed. "That was America then. There were no black people or Indian people like me." Then she pointed excitedly, seized with recognition. "Oh, look, there's one black person, a girl!"

It was as if she was seeing the beginning of a future that, decades later, would have room for her. I asked her what she meant when she said, "That was America then."

"It was more simple," she explained. "There was more racism, they didn't like the other people. But now that's changed. Now in Flushing High School we have black people and Indian people."

"Do you think they get along?"

"Sometimes they do."

Farida was not looking at that old image of America for who she ought to be. She is secure in her own identity as a Muslim. America is a place she has come to; it doesn't threaten the core of her being. This is what allows her to stay a little separate from her school friends, who are both immigrant and native-born. School is for talk of exams, homework, SATs. Her private thoughts remain at home, with her mother, her family. Of the other students, she remarked, "They don't ask me that much about my family. They don't ask, What does your father do, mother do? We just talk about school here."

"Do you want to talk about other things?"

"No, I don't. It's better. I can talk about my family to my close friends, people who are close to me. Not to other people; I don't like that."

For the first time I understood a deeper meaning for the head covering; it can be a line between private and public, a sign of inner strength. I was aware that, even in talking to me, Farida kept part of herself in reserve, shielded from the prying eyes of a stranger. Unlike many other teenagers, she had no need to bare herself, to confess and reveal all her secrets. Restraint and self-control—this is what Farida cherished.

"Who is closest to you?"

Farida let out a sigh and said in a soft voice, "My mom."

Her words coming out in a rush, she giggled as she described a very devout, skinny woman with fair skin. "She is good." Then she burst out laughing. "To me, at least." She went on, "I talk to her about everything. School, teachers, colleges. *Everything.* She listens *very carefully.*"

Here was the deepest source of Farida's strength: her mother, the woman who wove together tradition and aspiration. She embodies everything her daughter holds dear:

morality, kindness, sacrifice. Farida learned the values of Islam through her mother, who daily gave her advice, kept up her spirits when she faced difficulties at school. Her father was more outgoing and excitable, her mother cautious and reflective. "My mom is kind of different than other people. She doesn't talk to all the people. She thinks a lot before she does something. She is calm and quiet and thinks and then she does it."

Farida's mother often confided in her about herself, and the difficulties of her life. Farida's mother and father grew up in the same village in Bangladesh, though they came from very different circumstances. Farida's mother was from a well-to-do family and her father grew up poor. Yet Farida's mother was pleased when her match was arranged. Though her husband-to-be had no money, she saw in him some special qualities: he was considered quite brilliant, and had worked his way up through school to become an engineer.

"My father's family is lower than my mom's. It was kind of hard for her. My mother saw my father's personality, not the money, how much they had. She saw education, personality. He was a more responsible person. He had a good education in my country."

Still, Farida's mother regrets that she married so young—at sixteen, a year younger than Farida is now. "She told me that it's not fair, it's not a good life to get married so young. Now she wishes she could have been older, she could have been more responsible. She feels because she was young it was hard to be our mom."

After much probing, I had finally landed in the center of Farida's existence. Farida seemed like a still, calm pool, into which flowed so many currents: the story of two families, rich and poor, her father's brilliance, her mother's devoutness, and the new dreams they spun for their daughter in this strange new land. This is why Farida can get along in her unfamiliar surroundings: her mother affirmed the past, yet helped her daughter move into the future. "My mother says to me, 'I am here just for you. Not for me.'"

Farida, in turn, keeps moving ahead, very aware of the sacrifices and unhappiness her family has borne for her sake, and looks forward to the day when she will have her own job. "I can be on my own. I don't have to depend on other people. It gives me confidence, to be established. Because I like to be more independent. So I can do something for my family too. I can pay for them. Give them presents. I like to give to them. If I can." Once again she laughed, the same light sparkled in her eyes.

Nubaisha

PAKISTAN

Seventeen years old

"If you make me cry, I will make your whole family cry."

For Nubaisha's family, newly arrived from Pakistan, every day in the United States was torture.

Every day Nubaisha's mother complained of their home in College Point, New York, "What kind of house is this? This is like a servant's quarter. How can we live here, with all the children?"

Every day, on her way to school, Nubaisha would pass a group of American teenagers on the corner who taunted and cursed her. As a Pakistani Muslim, Nubaisha usually wore a veil over her head and a *shalwar kamize*—a long tunic and trousers underneath. In College Point, which still remains a largely white and Catholic enclave of brick and shingle houses and apartment houses, this made her stick out, a target of verbal attacks.

"When I wear my country's dress, and I go outside, everyone curse me, like 'F' word, like very bad word. At that time just my parents told me, 'Don't say anything.' Because I was new, and I don't know English that well, I always keep quiet. I walk very slowly, just like our country we do, 'cause we don't have to run fast."

"What kinds of things would they say to you?"

" 'Asshole.' 'Get out of our country.' 'You are stupid, how come you are here?' 'Hey you, Gandhi, Hindu, your god is bullshit.' At that time I want to hit him, but I can't, because everything is problem here."

Every day at school, Nubaisha cried, for the taunts did not end at the corner. She made friends with other South Asian teenagers, but they could also be gossipy and mean. Soon Nubaisha became a target of their jeers. Cruelty seemed to come from all directions—especially from boys, who complained that Nubaisha was very proud because she never talked to them.

Nubaisha is a heavyset girl with a round, childlike face and soft eyes. She laughs easily, in hearty bursts. But inside she is steely with pride. The daughter of a former major in the Pakistani army, Nubaisha is easily given to defending herself, to fighting back when someone dares to cross her.

In Pakistan, where governments totter, a prime minister and political leaders have been assassinated, and corruption is rampant, the army seems to be the only enduring force. It is both respected and feared. Nubaisha led a privileged life as the daughter of an army officer; she and her two brothers and two sisters moved all over the country. They always lived in large houses, with many servants. Their last house in Faisalabad had several rooms, including a guest room, a maid's room, and a large terrace where her mother used to sit out all day. "When we went to school, our servant carried our bag to the bus. We had one servant to wash

Nubaisha

our clothes, for laundry; one servant for cooking; one servant for cleaning the home," Nubaisha explained.

Her father, though, was not well and decided to retire from the army and open a clothing factory. For a while, the family continued to enjoy their upper-middle-class life. But then, due to a political shift in Pakistan, the family's fortunes went downhill. Everyone advised Nubaisha's father to emigrate, since he had three young daughters whose dowries he would have to pay. Nubaisha's elder sister was almost of age to be married, and they needed to buy the crockery and linens and household items for her betrothal. So Nubaisha's father applied for and received a visa, then set off for the United States with his elder son. Nubaisha, her mother, and her younger siblings followed a year later.

After the grand surroundings of their house in Pakistan, their new home in the States was a shock. The entire family—Nubaisha, her two brothers, one sister (her elder sister had married), mother, father, and uncle—crammed into a small three-room apartment in College Point, Queens. Nubaisha's mother desperately wanted to go back, often fell sick, and was operated on several times for a hernia, since she was not used to manual labor. "Here we have to do everything for ourselves," Nubaisha said. "My mother is from the army and she doesn't know how to cook that much."

The best work Nubaisha's father could find was as a limousine driver, which he hated. Nubaisha saw how her father's pride had been damaged, and she too felt the loss and shame. The whole family sank into regret about coming to America. "Over here people don't care about the army. In Pakistan, if my father's going to walk and they didn't salute, my father can curse them, and maybe slap them. That's the rule. He has great respect over there. Even in factory everyone scared; he is a major, they got to be careful in front of him. They have different rules in front of my father."

For some immigrant families, coming to the United States is like falling off a pedestal. They go from high to low, respect to disrespect. Everything they once enjoyed—status, wealth, comfort—is gone. Everything they took for granted in their native country—a nice house, clothes and schooling for their children—is now harder to obtain. For people like Nubaisha's family, each encounter in America can be a wincing blow, a reminder that they are no longer who they once were.

In some ways, though, Nubaisha could be any teenage girl who had a rough time socializing and was picked on by boys. Still there was more to it. Attending school with boys was completely alien to her. Like many traditional Muslim girls, Nubaisha had been raised not to talk to boys, not to look them in the eye or shake their hands. Her own elder sister, when she met her husband-to-be, did not even look him in the face until they were married. Whereas some immigrant Muslim girls slowly learn to mingle in a coed environment, for Nubaisha the shock of an American school was too much. Her only recourse was her pride. This was not only how she asserted who she was, but how she protected herself and covered her own hurt feelings. Nubaisha's parents were not particularly strict with her— they encouraged her to be friendly at school, so as not to call attention to herself. Nubaisha, though, retreated into herself, and declared again and again that she did not speak to boys.

"I have my own rules," she explained. "I never talk to guys. Whenever they ask me any question, I just answer."

Unfortunately, Nubaisha's refusal to talk to boys—especially South Asian boys—was seen as excessive pride. The more she ignored the boys, the more they taunted her.

Nubaisha had made friends with one Indian girl, whom her family did not approve of. "She's not a good girl; she has many boyfriends. She changes her boyfriends like she changes her clothes. Everyone thinks maybe I'm like her. My family said, 'Don't hang around with her. She make your reputation go down.' "

The brother of her friend began to taunt her. For two days in a row, he called her "Fat Girl." On the third day, the threats grew more extreme; he threatened to rape her and make her pregnant. Inside, Nubaisha was furious and pained, but she refused to show it. "You're going to get it," he called out to her. "I'm going to open your buttons and the rest of your clothes. You're going to be here in school and no one will find you and you won't be able to come out because you won't have any clothes on."

Nubaisha's face quivered, and another boy sneered, "Oh, look. She's going to cry."

At this Nubaisha whirled around. "I will not cry," she told him.

They laughed and cursed her again.

"Be careful," she told the boy who started the trouble. "I'm very dangerous. If you make me cry, I will make your whole family cry."

When he continued to curse her, she repeated her warning. "Remember this: you make me cry today and I will make your whole family cry."

The boy's taunts struck at Nubaisha's deepest feelings. No matter how far down her family had fallen; no matter how small their house, or how poor her English; no matter that she'd learned to wear jeans and let her hair loose, she was still a proud, upper-middle-class Muslim girl, the daughter of an army major, who would not lose face. "He probably thinks I don't know English, he can embarrass me. But because I was in the army, I know how to behave."

That night she told her parents what had happened. Her father went to the boy's house and told his parents that if their son dared insult his daughter he would hurt them. "Be careful," he warned. The father also went to the dean's office and demanded they punish the boy. The school administration saw the situation differently; Nubaisha was also involved in the fight, and the teacher did not appreciate Nubaisha's father's taking the matter into his own hands. This astonished Nubaisha. "I'm a girl; they embarrass me in front of everyone," she said. "I have to come to this school every day. I have to do something for myself."

For Nubaisha, America was an assault on everything she knew. There were the boys on the corner and the boys at school, the sight of her father in despair over his lowly work. It still shocked her that the things that had once propped her up—status, respect, family standing—counted for nothing in the States. She was raised to believe that she and her family had the right to fight back when insulted. Above all, they must not be shamed.

"In our religion it's normal. If a guy says anything like that, they can do anything. But nobody in the school helped me. No one, not my teachers, nothing."

Living in the United States had become a war of mistrust, divided between those who opposed her and those who were her allies; those who might endanger her reputation and those who would protect her. The deep antagonism between Nubaisha and American teenagers lay on both sides. They did not tolerate her dress, and she judged them just as harshly. "Over here, American girls, they don't have any future," she told me. "They marry like three or four times." Her Muslim identity had become a brittle shield to fend off the daily insults and the teenage discomfort she felt inside.

Back at home, within her large, extended family, Nubaisha also had to jostle for her own place. With brothers and sisters and cousins all around her, it wasn't always easy to get attention. Nubaisha was always losing out to her cousin, the star in the family, who had immigrated a few years before her, always got good grades, and moved more easily between American and Pakistani culture. Her cousin was seen as quick and smart, and Nubaisha was teased for being slow and lazy.

"Everyone says, 'You should be like Ayesha.' And I'm like no." At school, she never went up to the blackboard for grammar exercises, for fear that the other kids from Pakistan and India would make fun of her and tell her cousin, who would in turn mock her in the family. "She always embarrass me in front of everyone." Her cousin often laughed at Nubaisha because she didn't know how to dress in American-style fashions. "She have Tommy

Hilfiger jacket, Calvin Klein shirt. I came here for study. I don't have to dress up like that."

Still, Nubaisha loved to visit her cousin's house, where her uncle seemed to take a special liking to her. She often arrived there on Friday and stayed throughout the weekend, to cook and make a special tea for everyone. One day, her uncle praised her for scoring a 73 on a test. Then he turned to his own daughter and scolded her for not doing better than an 81. Nubaisha felt hurt. "He doesn't expect anything from me. He thinks I'm nothing."

After that, she stopped going to their house. Around the same time, Nubaisha took a job at Dunkin' Donuts, a decision that marked an important shift in her life. Suddenly she was in an environment where she was useful and felt at ease. She learned how to interact with Americans, talk to strangers, work a cash register. "I don't even care about the money," she told me, and she gave her check to her mother. Nubaisha enjoyed work for the experience of being out of the house, on her own. Best of all, her job gave her a different role from the one she was stuck with in the family.

"Before, they say she is very lazy, she likes to sleep, she is fat. When my school start, everyone says, 'Now you going to quit the job.' I say, 'I'm not going to quit the job because of that.' After school I go there, I go home and do my homework, sometimes I cook meal, and my uncle is very surprised. 'She's the same girl who's very lazy?' "

"I get confidence because of job. Otherwise, in our religion girls are not allowed to do work. But I like to work, because in my family I'm the laziest person."

The very America that hurt and toughened Nubaisha also offered her some way out of the stereotypes she was locked into within the family. For many immigrant girls, work becomes the space where they can find some room for themselves. Like Nubaisha, they learn skills for interacting with Americans and show their families that they can help financially. Nubaisha's extra money came in handy because her father had decided to take computer courses. For the first time, he was starting to plan for a new future. Her family was moving out of its initial shock and regret, and Nubaisha was part of that change.

With her new job, home life also changed. She grew more opinionated. Her uncle often scolded her for not wearing a *shalwar kamize,* but this time Nubaisha was quick to retort, "I'm only home three or four hours. I have to sleep. I have to change for school, I have to change for work, I have to change for home. I don't want to change that many times. Don't make me change."

She even began to talk back to her cousin. "She told my uncle I am very rude now. I am different and I look like American." Nubaisha laughed, as if shrugging off Ayesha's remarks. "I'm not interested in her anymore. She was really surprised that I was answering back. I tell you, after job, I can speak out a little bit."

She added with a giggle, "In my family now they say I'm very rude."

Over time, an emboldened Nubaisha began to change in the outside world too. Nubaisha dropped her friend and made friends with a different Indian girl, one who was more like her—who didn't talk to boys and concentrated on her studies. Though her parents warned her "not to make her own language bad," when other kids would yell at her in the cafeteria she began to shout back. "Now I start to fight with them every time. When someone curses me, I curse them back. I curse them more than them." She gave one of her hearty laughs. "I have confidence."

The white kids are still there, on the corner. By now, Nubaisha is less afraid. "I know they jealous from my dress. I don't care if they're jealous of my dress."

Recently she passed them and they called to her, "You asshole, how come you wear that dress again? Get out of our country!"

This time, Nubaisha did not stay silent. "*You* asshole," she shouted back. "What kind of dress *you* wear?"

"Ashrat"   AFGHANI
Seventeen years old

"I'm on the other side. I don't want to go by the rules."

Once upon a time, when Ashrat was little, her mother and the other women in the village were getting ready to fetch water from the river. Ashrat grabbed a bucket and set off on her own. Frantic, her family searched everywhere for their little girl. Finally, a woman near the shore spotted her. Less than a year old, Ashrat was already walking, going her own way.

"I was always like this," she told me with a laugh. "I just had to disobey my mother. I always had to do the opposite. I don't know why."

Ashrat loves to tell stories. Stories are the link to her family, to her past, to the land left behind. Stories explain the distance she's traveled since she's come to the United States. Stories have also become the lies she needs to hide her life as a teenager in America. And with those lies Ashrat may lose everything she loves.

Fair-skinned, with dyed hair and a compact frame, Ashrat talks in a fast, tough patter. Her eyes are vaguely Asian, but her background isn't easy to place. Ashrat grew up mostly in the United States and was the first at everything: the firstborn in a large Afghani family, the first to go to an American school, and the first to protest to her family about wearing a head covering.

As a little girl, she wore her head covered but was relentlessly teased by the other kids, who would snatch the scarf off her head in the schoolyard. When she complained, her mother told her, "Who cares what they think? That's your religion. You should be proud." Finally, her parents relented and Ashrat stopped wearing the scarf.

When she was twelve, her family moved to a different area, giving Ashrat a chance to start anew and turn her back on her old, tough school. "I was tired of being a goody-two-shoes," she said. "Just seeing the other kids do everything bad, I had to just try it, see what it is."

Ashrat's family live by strong, traditional rules. After school, she must come home, help her mother with the cooking and cleaning, watch her brothers and sisters and help them with their homework. No friends, no phone calls, and especially no dating with boys was allowed. Her only socializing was at Afghani events, where she was expected to be quiet and respectful to her elders.

One of the reasons Ashrat's family are so strict is that they came from a small village. In immigrating, they faced the shock of city living, with its mingling of so many different people and lifestyles, its dangers and freedoms. Though Ashrat's family have been in the United States for sixteen years, they keep their sense of identity and wholeness by staying very close to their village roots, their network of Afghani friends and family. They do not want their daughter to join the larger stream of modern city life.

Through school, peers, TV, Ashrat had already entered the America her parents so feared. Inside her, a rebellion was brewing. "My parents pray five times a day. Always on the holidays and everything. I might not dress like it, or look like it, but we're really into it. My parents especially. Not me. I'm on the other side. I don't want to go by the rules."

Ashrat longed for friends—friends whom she could talk with, spill her thoughts and her feelings to. The same little girl who waddled off to the riverbank wanted to see what life was like on the other side.

In junior high, Ashrat began to make new friends, and sneaked off to their houses to hang out. Once she took one step away from her family, more were to come. "Until eighth grade, I never really knew about how to use the train and all of that. But when I got into the ninth grade, forget it. I knew how to get from one place to the other. How to talk, how to act, how to do all this stuff."

She started to cut classes to go to the movies, bowling, to a dance party, even to go out with boys. She'd stuff different clothes into her bag, duck into a restaurant, and change in the bathroom. When she received her report card, she'd white out the attendance record so her parents wouldn't know. The quiet, introverted girl teased for her head scarf was suddenly a fast-talking, quick-witted teenager who was learning the moves she needed to keep up her secret life.

"If you're always home and going to school, you don't know what's outside of this world. You don't know what other people are and what they do. When I used to cut, go to my friends' houses, my boyfriends' houses, I found out how their families were. I thought I was the only one with problems. When I went to other people's houses, it's like every kid has their own little problem."

Ashrat was so driven to get away from the dreary, sealed-in life of home and school that she didn't know what she was running toward, exactly. She knew only how to push forward, determined to flee her parents' strictness. Yet her sheltered family life had not prepared her for the outside world. Her sense of judgment wasn't very good. She often befriended people who betrayed her—in a few months, a girlfriend and her sister would steal thousands of dollars from Ashrat's apartment—money her father had saved to buy a restaurant with his brothers. A boyfriend's parents were drug dealers. One day she was at his house and watched the cops drag his addict sister to a mental institution. Though she was troubled by these events, for Ashrat everything was exciting, even if it was disturbing too.

Back at home, Ashrat continued to attend Afghani events and to sit quietly and offer short, respectful responses any time one of the grown-ups spoke to her. But inside she was silently counting the minutes before she could escape. "I have two personalities," she explained. "When I'm around my family and everything, I'm real quiet. I give them yes and no answers. I don't give them full sentences. I don't let them know how I am. They're like, 'Oh, she's so sweet. She's an angel.' But my mother knows that I'm bad. In my family, there's always a black sheep, and I'm the one. She knows it."

Ashrat was in the middle of a full-blown rebellion, one that was also a rejection of the Afghani world she'd grown up in. She steered clear of other Afghani kids, for fear that they would gossip about her. "I know the way they are," she told me. "They're big mouths, that's for sure. They gossip a lot. When I was little, my family would put me near the elders, and they used to gossip all the time. I see the teenagers, they do the exact same thing. They'd be like, 'Oh, that girl has a boyfriend, she's like a slut.' They make themselves look good, and make the girl like she's a lowlife. I don't want to hang out with them. I just hold myself back."

She especially kept away from Afghani boys. "I don't like Afghani boys. If you go out with an Afghani guy, then after you dump them they're going to be like, 'Oh, she's a slut too. Who knows, maybe before me she went out with ten guys.' And your reputation will be ruined."

She found herself drifting more toward Hispanic kids; she liked their attitudes, the way they dressed, what she felt was a freer and easier way of behaving. Often Ashrat was mistaken for Puerto Rican, which she claims offends her. At home, her mother had picked up on the changes and was especially enraged that Ashrat hung around with Hispanic kids. "You act like you're more Spanish or more black," her mother complained. Playing at being Hispanic gave Ashrat a cover. Now she could be a bit cocky, quick with the comebacks, scornful of other Afghanis. She had a language for criticizing her culture. Blending in with her Dominican and Puerto Rican friends meant she could distance herself from her background.

"You're smart," her mother would often tell her, "but you go on the stupid side." At one point Ashrat's parents tried to pull her back by arranging a marriage with a cousin. The young man came to the house to look her over, but Ashrat once again rebelled, and talked back with fast and cruel words. "I just thought marrying your cousin is a big, wrong idea. And another thing, he had bad breath. So that was two strikes right there. Three, he was the same height as me. And he's older than me, and I didn't like that." Ashrat made a scene before her father, complaining, "How am I supposed to sleep with this guy next to me? I'm not going to have kids with him and I'm not going to have sex with him. You know I can't even think about kissing him." Her father was so embarrassed he dropped the matter.

One of Ashrat's steps toward freedom was to take a job as a cashier at a local supermarket. There, she quickly made friends with the manager, who would lie for her when she wanted some free time, arriving a few minutes before her mother came to pick her up. Ashrat took on shifts every afternoon after school and worked a double shift—fourteen hours—on Saturdays and Sundays. Even with the long hours standing on her feet and punching a cash register, Ashrat was happy. Compared with staying home, where she felt nagged by her mother or had to cook and clean and help her brothers and sisters, working at the store was even a little glamorous. There were other girls to talk to, a whole social world of friends.

And, best of all, there was a guy.

Soon after Ashrat began working at the supermarket, she met a man who was a manager at another store. Usually, Ashrat went out with a boy for a month or two—"for my pleasure"—and then broke up with him. This time, something in Ashrat softened. He wasn't like the boys she'd flirted with or gone out with. He was older, for one, and he treated her differently. Mornings, he would pick her up from school, and instead of going to classes they went out for big breakfasts at fancy restaurants. They spent time in a nearby park and took trips into the city and once even went horseback riding. Sometimes they went to hotels to be together. He seemed serious about her; he listened to her talk about her problems with her family. Most of all, he offered her what her family could not: the sense of being important. "He treats me nice. He babies me a lot. He makes me feel special." They even began to fantasize about a future together. He offered to get an apartment for them, and they talked about getting married and having a baby.

But her boyfriend had three strikes against him too: he was Puerto Rican, he was almost twice Ashrat's age, and he was married.

Ashrat had crossed to the other side, and that landed her

in more trouble and more heartache than she'd ever imag-
ined. When we first talked, she knew her mother was clos-
ing in on her. At the supermarket one day, her mother
noticed Ashrat talking to the guy, and hounded her with
questions about whether she was going out with him.
Ashrat denied it. "You can lie to me, but God's watching,
God's watching," her mother scolded. "You can do whatever bad you want to do, but at the end you're going to get
it." In the meantime, her boyfriend told her his marriage
was ending, and that his wife wanted out too.

Her mother made it very clear that she would disown
Ashrat if she dared to marry outside of her culture. " 'Even
if I see you across the street,' my mother warned, 'and you
came up to me, I'll spit at your face and I don't even know
you. I don't care if you're dying right then, I wouldn't even
come to your funeral.' I don't want that. I don't want her to
disown me. I want her to be there when I need her."

Ashrat's eyes filled with tears, and she could barely finish
what she was saying. It was as if she saw the image of her
mother on the other side of the street, lost to her. She told
me she was haunted by the memory of her old boyfriend's
sister being dragged off by the police to a mental institution. To her, that was a symbol of how bad it could get
when you go too far. She took a deep breath. "The way our
family is, you have to marry your own race. If you don't,
you'll be known as a slut and a bad family. And I don't want
that. I don't know what to do. Should I leave home and get
married to him? I'm just stuck there."

"Is it hard, keeping up the split life?"

"It's not hard. It's just, sometimes, your past catches up
with you. I'm just afraid that it's going to catch up with me."

A couple of weeks later, Ashrat's life exploded.

One day, her mother found a pair of boots under Ashrat's bed. She stormed into school, clutching the boots, and wanted to know how her daughter could have bought such expensive clothing. Once there, she learned about Ashrat's cutting classes. That day, she marched to the shoe store with Ashrat in tow, and demanded to know how the clerks could sell these "hooker boots" to a young girl. In front of the baffled clerks, she slashed the boots to pieces.

Ashrat was humiliated, but that was not the end of it. It was only a matter of time before her mother found out about Ashrat's boyfriend. "He's Spanish, he's a different culture," her mother told her. "You can't be Spanish, because you are Muslim. You can't change what you are. You could try as much as you can, hang out the way they do, drink, and, you know, change your entire attitude, your clothing, but you'll still be the same person. Nothing will change."

Her mother told Ashrat to quit her job when the week was up. A few days later, she called Ashrat at work and demanded to know whether she had slept with her boyfriend. Ashrat kept trying to avoid the question until, finally, she admitted that she had slept with him twice. Fifteen minutes later, her mother burst into the supermarket and ordered her to leave. Waiting outside were two policemen: Ashrat's mother had called the cops and asserted that her daughter had been raped. They took Ashrat to the hospital, though she privately told the policemen that she had not been raped. Her boyfriend was brought into the station for questioning, and then let go.

Days of angry scenes followed. What if I was pregnant? she asked her mother, who replied, "Just because you're pregnant, you think I'm going to let you be with that guy? No. You're going to have an abortion right away. You're not keeping this guy's child. I don't care." Her father, furious and pained, called relatives in Afghanistan to see about arranging a marriage for his daughter with a twenty-seven-year-old cousin. They might even take her to a doctor to have her hymen reattached. "They'll do it," she told me. "That's what happened to my cousin, only she got to marry the guy because he was Afghani."

It was over. The walk on the other side had ended. "I cried for three days straight," she told me. "Every time she threw it in my face—Oh, you know, you're a disgrace to the family—I started crying. Then, suddenly, I had no more tears."

Ashrat's rebellion wasn't just about wanting to taste danger, or checking out the other side. It was the only way to break from what she sees as the injustices in her culture. To date a Hispanic guy was a way out of a life she doesn't want to have. She knew, inside her, having been raised with traditional Muslim values, that everything she was doing would shame her family. The "spoiling" of a girl's virginity, her protected sexuality, is the worst shame her family could endure. It was also Ashrat's weapon against her parents and everything she felt stifled by.

The last day I talked to Ashrat, she was very subdued. She looked shaken; real fear showed in her eyes. Her two lives had crashed together and exploded. And she had no idea what to do. Despite everything, Ashrat is powerfully attached to her family. "I love my mother," she told me several times. "I don't want to lose her. I will always choose my family over a guy."

Ashrat's boyfriend has not given up. Not long after the confrontation at the supermarket, he called her in secret and pleaded with her to stay with him. When she told him that her parents would disown her if she went with him, he insisted that he would take care of her, and even offered to get her an apartment. And when he heard the news that her father was thinking of arranging a marriage, she told me he said, "I don't think so. No, you're mine, and I'm not going to let you get married to somebody else." Ashrat seemed to relish that he was fighting over her, declaring her his. After she revealed the fight with her parents about a possible pregnancy, he responded, "If I knew you were having my kid, you're not going to have an abortion. That's my kid and you're having it. I don't care if your parents are going to disown you, you're not going to take my baby's life away."

In many ways, Ashrat's boyfriend is no different from her parents: he is fighting for possession of her. He isn't seeing that she's an Afghani girl who, for better or worse, lives by the wishes of her family, and can't be separated from her mother. Her mother, on the other hand, can't see that Ashrat isn't just a vessel for the family's pride and tradition. Neither is seeing Ashrat for herself.

Recently, Ashrat has been obsessed with another story. Her mother called her sister overseas and asked that a village woman read Ashrat's future in the tea leaves. The old woman read the leaves and told Ashrat's aunt to be careful, for her niece was doing something bad. There was going to be a terrible conflict in the family, she predicted; someone would come for Ashrat's hand in marriage, and by June 2000 she would be married. Ashrat can't stop thinking about those tea leaves. "Oh my god, I'm really scared. I know it can't be this Hispanic guy, because I can't be married to him. Who is this guy? Who am I going to marry?" she asks over and over, as if she's staring into the brown smudges, trying to find the face of her future husband.

A few weeks after this conversation, Ashrat came to school wearing a head covering.

Mariwat

Seventeen years old

> *"I am trying to talk to people, to look in their eyes.*
> *And not to be afraid."*

When Mariwat boarded a plane taking her from Ethiopia to the United States, she never looked back. She had no regrets, no sadness about leaving her homeland. Behind her were only the ravages of war—the sight of beggars, broken-down streets, empty store shelves. Of all the teenagers I interviewed, Mariwat was the happiest to be here.

Mariwat attends Fairfax High School, in downtown Los Angeles. As I drove into the parking lot, the school seemed to me to resemble a movie theater; a lit-up sign announced the evening classes as if they were a coming feature attraction. Fairfax has become a magnet for immigrant teenagers. Upstairs, on the second floor, in the narrow shoebox room of the ESL office, immigrant teenagers traipsed in and out; a Russian girl and her mother answered questions for a placement interview; student volunteers answered phones and dealt with questions.

Into this noisy hubbub stepped Mari, as she is known here, a shy, soft-spoken girl whose hair is done in neat cornrows. Her clothes were adult-looking, almost prim: a long leather jacket, a loose rayon vest with matching trousers, and white heels. She spoke in careful, halting phrases, and took sudden deep breaths between sentences, as if she were

Mariwat

gulping down her words. We talked in Fairfax's courtyard, perched against the concrete planters for shrubbery.

Our conversation was very brief, and yet, afterward, Mari lingered in my mind. Perhaps it was the sweet trust-fulness that shone in her eyes, her quiet, self-contained manner. Even in her short answers, she conveyed such simple and strong emotions. Mari is in that in-between space of recent immigrants: she is experiencing a great deal, but doesn't have the language to express it. Though I could barely reach inside that space, or touch all the details, I could feel how she was brimming over with new thoughts and sensations. And even in her basic English, one thing came across: her profound relief at being here. Mari seemed dazed by her good fortune. Now and then, she glanced around at the blue California sky, the palm trees and hedges, as if to check that they were real.

"In my country was war," she told me. "There is no peace. Everything is very bad. There was not enough food. Scarce of wood. There are so many poor peoples, they beg on the street, they have no home, they are homeless. So terrible. I didn't like to see."

Mari was raised by her uncle and barely knew her own father, for he had left more than a decade before in search of work. Of her mother she said very little, only that she knew her but didn't live with her. Her father, meanwhile, went first to the Sudan, then to Greece, where he met Mari's stepmother. The two immigrated to the United States and settled in Los Angeles. Life wasn't easy at first. They had money problems, difficulty with English, and trouble finding jobs. They now live in a house in the Fairfax area; her father owns two cabs and her stepmother works as a nurse.

Life for Mari in Ethiopia was lonely and difficult. She took comfort in the church—every day, after school, Mari went to services and classes. (The Coptic Ethiopian Orthodox Church dates back to the fourth century.) Mari loved the stories the priest would tell.

"In my country, you have to work by yourself," she told me. "You're left alone. It's hard to understand. They don't explain. They don't care about students."

The news that she would join her father came as a surprise, but she was also eager to go, even if, underneath, she was terrified by the prospect of living with a strange new stepmother. When Mari's father met her at the airport, he was crying, stunned by his grown-up daughter. And at home, to Mari's delight, she discovered her father and stepmother had a newborn baby girl. Better yet, her stepmother was kind and welcoming. For Mari, it was almost a fairy tale come true.

Mari's eyes welled with tears when she talked about her stepmother. She is very aware that her fate might have been totally different if they had not gotten along. "I like her very much," Mari whispered. "She is not like others, she treats me very well. She is a good person."

For Mari, the transition into her father's new family has been smooth. Once she was alone, and now she is surrounded by parents and a baby sister. She relishes this new bounty in her life. Every morning, her stepmother leaves to go to the hospital, her father to drive a cab, and she to school, while the baby is taken care of by an Ethiopian babysitter. Mari loves her classes, the other students who come from all over the world. "It's really good, because we know all cultures. I like that. We have a similar level of speaking. We aren't ashamed to speak."

Mari has already made a best friend, Kochu, from Korea, who is in the same ESL classes. After school, she walks home with two other Ethiopian students, washes the dishes, and watches her baby sister. After dinner, she studies. On weekends, her father sometimes takes them for long drives around Los Angeles; so far, her favorite place is a building on the UCLA campus. Mari hopes to become a dentist, since she is good at math and science.

Both her father and her stepmother have taken charge of Mari's life, and made it very clear that they are raising her in the United States, not Ethiopia. They offer advice based on their own experiences and on their observations of other immigrant Ethiopians; they tell her to focus on her studies and not to get distracted. "If you don't work hard, life will be difficult for you," they warn her. Too often, they explain, they have watched people from their country fritter their time and money away, only to have hardships later.

They have only one rule for her: don't hang around with other Ethiopian kids, don't speak to them in Amharic, for you won't learn English. Mari showed little regret over this lack of contact with other Ethiopians her age. "I don't give my telephone number to other Ethiopian students," she told me. She has also noticed that Ethiopians act differently in Los Angeles; they will rarely acknowledge one another in public.

Mari's focus is on adapting to a culture that treats children and teenagers in unfamiliar ways. She's not used to the freedom, the boldness of American kids. "In my country, they punish, sometimes they kill their children. They are so cruel. Here the children have freedom. If family spank them, they ask the police. In my country there is no one. So the children are afraid to talk back, afraid to say what they want."

The hardest thing, she explained, is learning to look people in the eye. In Ethiopia, children are expected to keep their gaze averted. Mari practices the direct stare of Americans, but it is not easy for her. I could see this even as we talked. She would tilt her head, as if surprised that I showed an interest in her, worried that she had given the wrong answer.

"It's difficult for me to change," she said, with a timid smile, "but I try to change myself. I am trying to talk to people, to look in their eyes. And not to be afraid."

Andre
Eighteen years old

YUGOSLAVIA

When I was twelve, I had to leave Sarajevo suddenly. In five hours, we had to take our clothes and we had to move. I had no idea where we were going. We were going to Belgrade first. It was unusual. I didn't know what happened. I thought we were going to Belgrade for one week. Then we will come back. I didn't say nothing to my friends. I never came back to say goodbye. I stayed there two, three months. Then we went to Frankfurt, Germany.

In the beginning in Germany it was hard. I had to immediately start learning in German. The people are different. In Yugoslavia, the people are relaxed. In Germany, they work hard, they are not so relaxed. In the beginning they were not friendly. But then it became easier. I made friends. I was sad when I had to leave Germany. It surprised me.

But we couldn't stay in Germany. All the refugees had to go back to Yugoslavia. We didn't want to go back: the city was destroyed and the people are different in Sarajevo. They are from villages, they are not the same people in the city.

This school in the United States is the easiest. I don't learn nothing. It's like it's fifth grade in Yugoslavia.

I think about Sarajevo. I miss the friends, we played on the streets. The neighborhood—there were a lot of kids, I had a lot of friends. Now I have one friend in San Pedro, I travel one hour to see him. Now I will stay here. I don't know what will happen in two or three years. In Germany, I couldn't do any jobs because I was a foreign citizen, I couldn't go to the police. Here I can do everything.

Kaying

Eighteen years old

"If you make one mistake, that's the end of your teenage life."

In his gray sweatshirt and bleached jeans, Kaying looks like all the other clean-cut kids I had seen on the snowy streets of Madison, Wisconsin, a funky college town in the heart of the Midwest. All Kaying wants to be is another normal American teenager. But for Kaying, this is not so easy. He is a double immigrant, with double vision. He must keep one eye on America and the other on his Hmong family and clan.

The Hmong are nomadic mountain people from the mountains of Laos, who, despite many invasions and wars, have preserved their culture. During the war in Southeast Asia, they fought the communists, but were driven from their villages and forced to live in refugee camps on the border of Thailand. There, families stayed for many years, crowded into cement-block buildings, their lives in limbo. Some waited for peace, so they might return to their homes. Others hoped to immigrate to Thailand. Over time, several church groups sponsored Hmong families for resettlement in the United States, particularly in the Midwest.

The resettlement of Hmong in these communities has not always gone easily. Often, the towns were tight-knit, all-white enclaves where not much had changed since an

Kaying

earlier set of immigrants, from nineteenth-century Germany and Scandinavia, came to farm the lush, open countryside. The Hmong are also a tight-knit people, having lived for centuries in remote mountain villages where they practiced long-established customs. Their culture is oral, which means they pass down knowledge through stories and songs, and they produce beautiful appliqué work. Though all this makes for a rich heritage, it also meant that the Hmong were forced to adjust to a very different society, in which reading and writing are essential to survival.

The Hmong teenagers are unique in being "double immigrants." Many of them were born in the camps and know their homeland only through stories told by their parents and grandparents. Though many of the Hmong teenagers are hardworking and disciplined, others have gained a reputation for joining gangs. The gap between Hmong parents, raised with ancient traditions, and their children, brought up on an American TV culture of strip malls and dating, is huge. By American standards, Hmong parents can be very strict; children must respect their elders and are sometimes beaten if they disobey.

I met Kaying on a cold March day. He spoke haltingly, but always with a certain firmness and self-control. He has clearly found strength in solid school activities, including sports, academics, and cultural clubs. Beneath the all-American image lay another strength: Kaying is an elder son, a very important responsibility in the Hmong community, and he has an elder son's bearing.

Born in a camp in Thailand, Kaying remembered it as a place where families had nothing to do. For a while, his father was the director and teacher of a workshop that sewed items for sale and export, one of the few ways

Hmong could earn a living. Kaying went to school from an early age and quickly advanced; by the age of eleven, he was one year away from becoming a teacher.

"In a way it was fun," he explained, "but in a way scary, because you really don't have any kind of power or rights. Those Thai people, they can do anything to you and you can't do anything about it."

This awareness of individual rights crops up again and again in Kaying's talk. Maybe it was the trauma of the war; of living year in and year out in cinderblock houses surrounded by wire fences, belonging to no country. Kaying has experienced what it's like to have no official status or citizenship. He's determined to plant himself firmly in the country and the institutions that will protect his rights as a citizen.

"We had three choices: Stay in the camp. Go to the border and move back someday. My mom say, 'It's better that we come to America, because there's more opportunity, there's more education. If we stay here, the life's not going to be that different. But if we go, the kids' life will be different.'"

Kaying's family moved swiftly into the mainstream. In Wisconsin, Kaying attended ESL classes, then was quickly shifted into a regular program. His father trained as a computer programmer, while his mother found work on an assembly line in a factory. When he entered high school, though, small conflicts erupted between him and his parents. Kaying had begun to look like an American kid, with baggy jeans and long hair. In a culture of respect and obedience to elders, Kaying was testing the limits of his parents' tolerance. He, in turn, resented that they did not trust him more.

"Freshman year, they always want me to stay home, because they think I'll get into gangs and things like that.

I'm telling them, I'm one of those persons who knows the limit. I'm not crossing the line.

"Right now they think I'm kind of bad, just because I grow my hair like this. Like, if my friend wears baggy clothes or grow their hair out, then they say those friends are bad. But it's not like that. If you have trusting and honest friends, those are good friends. In many ways, our interpretation of good kids is different than our parents'. My mom thinks the way a person dress, the way a person lifestyle is, determines his personality. I don't really believe in that."

Kaying's manner began to change. I saw the teenager emerge from the slightly stiff, responsible young man, as if he were shedding a skin. His sentences were dotted with more Americanisms, "like" and "stuff," his inflection becoming that of someone "cool" and part of a crowd. He wasn't trying to impress me as much; he was giving me a glimpse of who he was when with his friends.

In wanting to wear the clothes he liked, Kaying was no different from any other American teenager. Underneath his complaints, though, lay a difference: he was hurt that his parents judged him by his appearance. He was calling out, "I'm still the same Hmong boy who could have become a teacher in the camps. I'm still your responsible elder son." His hurt is almost philosophical. He might flirt and play with American fashion, but he still holds on to his core identity.

Even a normal American teenage activity like sports causes tensions in Kaying's family. A passionate soccer player, Kaying pours his energies into the varsity team and a self-organized Hmong team, though he does so without the approval of his parents. Here in this Midwestern college town, where parents drive their kids to Little League practice to cheer from the bleachers, and athletes are local heroes, sports have been a strangely isolating experience for Kaying.

"All the Hmong parents, they don't really support the athletic activities I participate in. In their opinion, it's just like a waste of time. I play soccer for my school for three years and my parents don't really come to my games."

Then there's an even more serious problem: dating and girls. Hmong boys can't take for granted the casual hanging out and dating that's such an integral part of American teenage life. "In Hmong culture, you can't go up to parents and say, 'I'm going to take your daughter to a movie' or 'I'm gonna take her to a party,' " Kaying explained, "because in Hmong culture, somehow, if kids are alone by themselves, then they start doing bad things."

"Is dating allowed?" I asked.

"It's allowed, but if you make one mistake, that's the end of your teenage life. If I took a car out to play with a girl and if she didn't get back before dark in her house, then, if her parents would just say, 'You have to marry her,' you can't say anything about that, it's a part of tradition."

I saw the map of Kaying's life, the constant zigzag between American teenage desires and Hmong expectations; between individual freedom and respect for his elders and family. Kaying and his friends invent strategies to win more freedom for themselves. If they want to spend time with a girl, they pick her up on the corner, away from her house, so the parents assume she's with her girlfriends.

College isn't a straight and easy path either, for Kaying must balance his own desires with his parents' expectations. "In American culture you can go to any school or do whatever you want," he explained. "The Hmong culture, they just want everything to be like the traditional stuff. Whatever your father do, follow him. My uncle, he finished high school and went to college in Madison. Right now my parents want me to go to UW Madison. But I was telling them that right now I got the opportunity to go to a better school. I could be something different than my uncle."

There are other obstacles to moving deeper into America besides his parents' rules. Each time Kaying has stepped from his protected environment, he has faced a less open, more hostile world, where he's often judged by his ethnicity and race.

"In school, I was able to do a lot of stuff. But outside of school, I can't really do anything. I can't really get a job that I want. I doubt I'll be able to get the same job as some white kid would. It makes me kind of mad. I'm an all-around student—I participate in the leadership club, mediation—but whenever I apply for a job I want, I can't get it. Some of those white students, all they do is come to school, they don't do anything else, they don't get good grades, and when they apply for a good job, they get it.

"Among all the Asian students, most of them have jobs, but in McDonald's, Burger King, and cleaning, and I would not like to work like that. 'Cause I know I could function at a different level, where I could use some skills, instead of using physical strength. I told them, 'If you settle for those jobs, in life you're going to settle for less than you're capable of.'"

When Kaying spoke of these incidents, there was hurt in his voice. America, the country of freedom and possibility and individual rights, was failing him. After the anarchy of war and the difficulty of being a refugee, he'd worked hard to become an American. Just as he wanted his parents to see he was a good kid even in his baggy clothes, he wanted employers to see his accomplishments, not his ethnic background. And so he is a careful reader of where real possibility lies for him. He has visited colleges, and assessed which ones offer the best job placements. Like many Asian immigrants, he is choosing to focus on math and science, because he knows he'll be more easily judged for his skills in those fields, rather than what he looks like.

I decided to end the interview by appealing to the student leader in Kaying, asking what his message would be to other students. He thought for a moment and said firmly, "Don't settle for less than what you're capable of. Be an open-minded person. Then your experience will be really valuable." He paused. Then, as if switching audiences, he addressed the world he wants to enter and added, "Be really open to people like me."

Gerson

Seventeen years old

I grew up in the capital on the largest island in Cape Verde. I lived with my grandmother, my father's mother. She raised me. I knew my mother too; she lived nearby and I saw her every day. My father left when I was nine months old. I didn't really know my father. I knew him in pictures.

When I was thirteen I came over with my father and my older brother and sister. Leaving my friends and my grandmother, that was the hardest thing. I have a stepmother, she's from Guatemala and she's really nice. My father works two shifts, as a supervisor of a motel and he works at a college. He works from eight till four and from six to ten on weekdays.

I love soccer. I love the game. I want to play professionally. I started playing when I was four years old. We used to play on the streets, 'cause we didn't have nets and stuff. We used to put two rocks over there, and two rocks over there, and when cars come we take it off. We didn't have the balls. We used to make balls from socks, tied together until it gets big. After we started growing up, we had balls and stuff like that. Still, there's no grasses either. When it's raining, you can't play 'cause it's all muddy.

I play on the soccer team my sophomore year and my senior year. This year we went to the finals. I was the second-highest scorer. I was named the all-star of the high school [in Cambridge], stuff like that. I'm going to be on a sports scholarship, that's what I'm working on with the coach. I want to study communications, media, TV, do sports journalism.

We practice every day. Our team, we have three kids from Brazil, four kids from Haiti, two from Ethiopia, one from Tanzania, one from El Salvador, one from Guatemala, one kid from Croatia, one from Ireland, and me from Cape Verde. Two, their family was born here.

Sports helps me. I used to get mad all the time. Like, I'd call something out, even with the teachers. Started arguing and stuff like that. Then I start changing. I don't do that anymore.

Most of my friends are from Cape Verde. I have a lot of friends who are American too. Cape Verde friends, I can tell them everything. My American friends, I say, What's up? It's not the same, it's not tight. My Cape Verde friends, we from the same place, we know each other. There's not a lot of difference between us. We listen to hip-hop and reggae and Cape Verde music. It's called zouk; it's originally from the West Indies, Guadeloupe and Martinique. It's like soca; it's like slower, though. With a rhythm—you can dance.

My father, he's strict, but I just tell him where I'm going, it's not a problem. He gives me advice all the time. Not to mess up. Not to go the wrong way. Don't do the bad stuff. He's always telling me the future, education is the key. I don't fight with him. There's no reason to. I don't want to hear the truth, but he's telling me the truth.

Vladislav and Victor

Fourteen years old and eighteen years old

"Here in America, teenagers do not have so much freedom."

"You must talk to Victor!" everyone exclaimed at Fairfax High, in Los Angeles, "you must talk to him!" Mrs. Ritter, head of the ESL program, told how Victor had appeared in a school performance as a woman and kept the entire audience roaring with laughter. The impression I was given was of a teenager different from the others, unafraid and uninhibited. Victor was simply himself.

On the day we were supposed to talk, though, Victor had to go to court about a car accident. I scheduled an interview with Vladislav, who also grew up in the Ukraine. At fourteen, Vladislav was the youngest teenager I interviewed. He looked as if he was just emerging from childhood, dressed in a striped shirt, shorts, and tube socks. At the same time, like many Russian teenagers, Vladislav was also very sophisticated and spoke excellent English. He had arrived only a month and a half earlier, and though he was eager to talk, he also resisted making any broad generalizations about what he'd experienced so far. "It's too soon," he kept insisting.

Immigration was a blow to Vladislav's parents, who were used to higher status back in the Ukraine. "It's hard to change life at this age, they are not young," Vladislav said thoughtfully. "My father is about fifty, my mother is forty.

Victor and Vladislav

My mom, she can only speak and say, 'I am Olga, I am forty years old.' " During our conversation, Vladislav echoed what many of the Russians and Eastern Europeans said: that school here was very easy. "I studied this program of math two years ago," he said. "That is one good thing in Ukraine, the knowledge we get from school, it is better. But in universities, it's not better."

In the middle of my interview with Vladislav, Victor came strolling across the courtyard, smiling, as if we had already met. He was dressed in a check-print blazer, and wore his hair in a ponytail. He seemed fully grown-up, relaxed, sitting among the California shrubbery. I could see the sharp contrast to Vladislav: not only was he older, but he seemed utterly comfortable in his surroundings.

My conversation with Victor was short, but intense and thoughtful, for he is a keen reader of cultural dynamics. He likes to muse on the differences between Americans and Russians, and offers unusual glimpses into questions of manhood and identity, freedom and independence.

Victor grew up in a picturesque thirteenth-century town in the Ukraine, not far from the Polish border. He knew every corner of his hometown: the cinemas, the libraries, the museums, the paths in the parks. His father was a professor of engineering and his grandfather was in the army, which meant they could not emigrate until five years after his grandfather retired. Finally, in 1994, they were able to leave.

"When I was young, it was my dream to go to the United States. A lot of my friends, they have families here. My friends told me a lot about America, that it's a very good life, everything is so good, you can do what you want. There are a lot of places to go—Magic Mountain, Disneyland."

"Once you came here, did it seem like everything you heard?"

"Actually, I was completely disappointed. Everything was different, the people were different."

Compared with most immigrant teenagers, Victor is remarkably at ease in this country. His English flows smoothly, though he says it was difficult in the beginning, since he, like all Russians, had learned British English and couldn't understand the American accent. Not only is he well liked at Fairfax High School, with plans to attend college and medical school, but he already has a regular job in a law office. He even has his own car. Victor, it would seem, has slid right into California life without a ripple of difficulty.

Inside, though, it hasn't all been easy. Like Vladislav, Victor has watched his parents' struggles. His father, an accomplished engineer and once the breadwinner in the family, stays at home all the time. "My father did not like it so much here, because in Russia he was a teacher in the university. Before he became a teacher, he studied for twenty-five years and went to many institutes. A lot of people know him and say he is a good teacher and respected. But here he knows nobody. He tried to get a job, but nobody will take him, because his English isn't so good. Now he is studying to try to make his English better. My father, he became more angry because I get a job, my mother get a job, but he didn't get a job."

The hardest thing for Victor, however, has been adjusting to the social life in a California high school. Victor was used to his friends back in his hometown, with whom he would range through the streets talking about life, the future.

"In Russia," he explained, "you can share your thoughts. Here, if you share with somebody else, they laugh at you. When I came here, I had a lot of friends. I told something to my friend. Later we had a fight. This friend, he told all my other friends what I told him. It was really bad, because I shared my feelings and after everybody knew my feelings. After that, I stopped sharing my feelings."

"Was he American?"

"Actually, the interesting part was he was a Russian teenager. When people come here they change really fast, and not in a good way. They become more in themselves, they do not like to help. In Russia, if you ask somebody to help or if you need help, people help you. In this way, you help everybody. Here, nobody will help you. They just care about themselves."

Victor doesn't easily fit into an American male "type." He is expressive, expansive, uninhibited, and full of opinions. He finds the conversations among teenagers strangely limited and superficial—all about dating and boys and girls, or how much money someone makes at a job. Victor craves deeper and more satisfying relationships, and has been baffled by the trouble he's encountered socially.

"Making friends has been the most difficult thing. I make friends and in two weeks we break up. Here I change a lot of friends already. We break up because of a lot of fights. About nothing. People just imagine things. For example, you go out with somebody else's girlfriend or you say something wrong. In Russia, I don't know why, I didn't have these problems."

The other aspect of teenage life in America that Victor finds puzzling is the relative lack of freedom. Whereas most people think American teenagers have more freedom, Victor believes the opposite is true.

"Here in America, teenagers do not have so much freedom. In Russian schools, nobody cares if you come to school or do not come. You need to get your knowledge by yourself. Here, teachers try to keep you in the class, to have gates to keep you in school. But actually people do not get so much knowledge."

The more we talk, the more it becomes obvious that, like Yulia, Victor is bumping up against the whole notion of "teenage." For Yulia, discovering teenage in the California landscape was liberating and fun. She could savor a prolonged childhood mingled with some adult freedoms. For Victor, to be a teenager in America has been a setback. Back in the Ukraine he'd grown used to his independence and the clear break he'd made from childhood. Coming to America meant losing all the privileges he'd had, especially as a young man.

"In Russia, you become a man when you get your passport at sixteen. You get your freedom. You can do whatever you want. Like, everybody goes to parties, they do not listen to their parents, they do whatever they want. Here it's a little bit different, because actually, by law, you grow up at twenty-one years. People are confused. They try to make fake IDs, to look bigger, to do things differently."

Victor also observes that in the United States it takes years and years to establish oneself. School takes up a much longer time, which means the "young-adult" period stretches interminably. "In Russia, you finish school in eleventh grade, and you finish university and get a good job. Here, for example, I want to be a doctor. I need to study thirteen years. Only up to that time will I feel like a man because I will get a good job."

By now, Victor and I were sitting at concrete tables in the lunchroom, a covered outdoor area where a maintenance man was sweeping up. While we were talking, Vladislav hovered nearby. He obviously wanted to catch Victor's attention; he tagged along like a younger brother, talking to Victor in Russian. There were jokes passed between them, and smiles. Victor was polite, but he did not keep up the banter for very long. It was a rare moment for me to see two immigrant boys—a newcomer and a more experienced immigrant—interacting with each other. I got some glimpse into what Victor had been speaking of when he talked of friendship and manhood: the affection between two Russians, the kindness Victor showed to a boy who was still groping for his place.

Maria

Seventeen years old

"I changed completely. From my head to my toe."

For Maria, coming to the United States meant arriving on the doorstep of a complete stranger, and becoming a stranger to herself.

Maria is beautiful, with ringlets of hair that cascade down her face, sly eyes, and a mischievous smile. She talks in a fast patter—part street tough, part Spanglish, though now and then a girlish vulnerability breaks through. She dares me to ask her tough personal questions, and then dares me again with her answers. Her laugh is wicked, half embarrassed, half challenging—a sudden *whoof*-noise she makes with her lips.

What I like about Maria is she's honest and has no illusions. She's theatrical, she wants attention, and she has found it through boys. Since she came to the States two years ago, she has learned to run with her looks; unfortunately, she's run too fast, and now she doesn't know how to get back where she came from. She went from being a quiet immigrant girl to a rebel who narrowly missed going to juvenile court, and she is now in a school for troubled teenagers.

How did this happen?

Maria's mother was only fifteen when she gave birth, and soon after gave up her child. Maria grew up reared by her

Maria

grandmother. She spent her childhood attending a strict Catholic school in Santo Domingo, where she wore a uniform and did pretty well in her classes. At fifteen, she was sent to live in Cambridge, Massachusetts, with a father she didn't even know. He, in turn, had married another woman, with whom he had two sons. Maria's father, though, kept two apartments and went to live with his new family on weekends.

This is a common pattern for immigrants from the Caribbean and Central America. Often, a mother or father will immigrate north, leaving the child in the care of another family member. For years, the parents know their son or daughter through photos, letters, and phone calls. When the child becomes a teenager, he or she is sent to the United States to get a better education. For teenage girls, this can be an especially difficult meeting. The parent, who may have remarried and had other kids, hasn't the faintest idea how to deal with this new stranger in the home. The innocent girl in snapshots and letters is suddenly a half-woman with opinions, struggles, and a budding sexuality. For these teenagers, immigrating isn't just about taking on a new country. It's about starting a new life with a new family.

Maria found herself all alone in a strange country living with a strange man and one of her stepbrothers. "It was bad, because I didn't really know my father—he just sent money to my grandmother. So it's kind of hard. We don't know each other really." She was lonely, for her father worked long hours as a machinist.

Her first few months, she stayed to herself. She missed her life in the Dominican Republic, its balance of comfort, strictness, and looseness; there, school let out in the early afternoon, and she was free to play or even to go to nightclubs with her girlfriends.

After a few months in the United States, Maria drifted into a crowd of Dominican and Puerto Rican kids, most of them born here. They asked to copy her homework, and she readily complied. To her, they seemed tough and experienced, and made fun of her dress, her hairstyle, and, most of all, her virginity. In the Dominican Republic, virginity was a prize girls cherished and held on to. But here Maria felt like a freak. She decided to catch up with them. Soon enough, she was outdoing the girls who mocked her.

"They're kind of different," she said of her new friends. "They do things, and then you start doing things because you want to be accepted. Before, I was so quiet. If someone tell me not to do something, I didn't do it. Now, if I want to do something, I just do it. I don't really care. I just want to have fun."

"What happened?"

"I guess peer pressure. Here, if you don't want to smoke, you don't want to cut class, they start laughin' at you, so you have to do whatever. So I start smoking and hanging out."

In the Dominican Republic, peer pressure meant something else—a check that kept her in line. If she did something wrong, a girlfriend would take her aside and warn her. Here, Maria found herself under pressure to keep up. Soon a normal teenage rebellion became extreme, since Maria was living with people with whom she had only the thinnest of connections. All the restraints that kept her in control were gone.

"I changed the way I dress and everything," she explained. "My hairdo, my earrings, everything. A lot of rings and everything. I changed completely. From my head to my toe. I changed so fast. My cousin was like, 'Damn, girl, you changed. I remember when you first came here.' My teachers are like, 'Oh my goodness.' "

Maria just wanted something to belong to, to replace what she missed. She didn't belong to her father and new brothers, and she didn't get along with her stepmother. At the same time, her father could not understand why Maria didn't do what she had come here for: to go to school and to take advantage of the opportunities in the United States. He wasn't prepared for a girl's needs, such as friends and parties.

More and more, Maria and her father began to fight. He set down the law: No boyfriends. Be at home by a decent hour. Come to your stepmother's every weekend. Maria was resentful; she felt she was holding up her end of the bargain by going to school, and she couldn't understand how this man whom she barely knew could deprive her of a social life. The fights became ugly; Maria would scream that she hated him, that he wasn't her father; he complained that one day she would give him a heart attack. "My father was always saying, 'I wish you'd never been born a girl.' "

The breaking point came over a friend's *quinceria* cele-bration—in the Dominican Republic, this is a party thrown for a girl who is fifteen, similar to a Sweet Sixteen party. Weeks before, Maria bought a special dress and a present. The day before the party, her father told her she couldn't go. Then came the big blowup. Maria threatened to leave; her father told her that if she did she'd better not come back. That weekend, clutching a bag of clothes, Maria climbed out of the second-story window of her stepmother's house and went out on the streets.

At first, she felt an exhilarating sense of adventure. Maria went from friend's house to friend's house, sleeping on couches and floors, doing as she pleased. After three days, her friends grew nervous and told her to leave, since they didn't want any trouble. Maria started to beg for a place to sleep from different boys she knew. Soon freedom gave way to something else, as the boys began to pressure her for sex. "They were supposed to be my friends, just friends," she said of the boys. "I stay there for a night and then I couldn't deal and so I went to another house. The girls didn't talk to me like they used to."

Maria had slipped from being a rebellious daughter to a "bad girl," easy prey for boys and shunned by the other girls. The dream of escape had become a nightmare of dead ends. To leave home, Maria learned, was to fall off the edge of respectability.

When immigrant girls rebel, their lives can quickly become very stark. Once a girl strays, she can't easily put herself back on track. Her reputation is ruined. There's no room to screw up, make mistakes, or go down the wrong path for a while. There are very few options left.

In Maria's case, rumors were spreading about her, particularly among the girls. Then Maria caught wind that someone had warned another girl that Maria wanted to fight her. In the whirl of confusion and betrayals, Maria showed up at school with a knife, ready to fight the girl who'd spread the rumor. She pushed her down a set of stairs; the security guards came running before Maria pulled the knife from her pocket.

Maria's short-lived adventure was over. The authorities took her home to her father, who was so angry he refused to talk to her for weeks. She was kicked out of her high school and sent to a school for troubled teenagers, a place she detests. Worst of all, she lost her "group," the friends she thought she could rely on, around whom she'd shaped her whole life. "I thought some of them were really my friends, and those were the ones who turned their back."

Now Maria is more alone than ever. "I'm kinda confused right now," she told me. "I don't trust anyone. I just want to be normal, go to high school," she said wistfully, several times.

Maria is also clearly fascinated with this swirl of "bad" talk about women. Of her own mother, she was told by her father that "she was a *puta,* a whore. She gave me to him when I was five months because she didn't want to have the responsibility." Maria hears from her father how "women are so bad, they are made for the kitchen and taking care of kids. The only good woman is his mom." She wants to play with being the "bad girl," because she knows it's the one thing that will enrage her father, get his attention. Half of her seems to believe it's her fate to flirt with danger; half of her is confused by the havoc she's created for herself. She doesn't know how, two years after coming here, she's wound up in a school for problem kids, in rooms of broken chairs, a pariah in her family, with little hope of a regular life.

In a funny way, her "badness" has won her a badge of power. She's the first to admit that she actually likes being whispered about by the other girls. She likes strutting by the other girls with her jewelry and her flashy eyes, knowing the boys are after her. It's become a game to her, a painful game, but one she's determined to play well.

"A lot of girls don't like me. They think that I'm going to wear whatever I have to do—"

"To get boys' attention?"

Gales of laughter fell from Maria's lips, as if she was relieved that I understood what she meant. She was embarrassed, but at the same time a bright wickedness sparkled in her eyes. She seemed glad to be able to say what she really felt, even if it was outrageous.

"When you hear things, like you hear, 'She's bad—' "

"That makes me feel good, actually. 'Cause that makes me feel like I'm so important. So I feel like, 'Oh, they're talking about me.' I mean, I know they're talking about things that I really did, but I don't really care if it's true. But if it's lying, that really hurts me."

"Do you have a boyfriend?" I asked.

"Now I have many boyfriends." She let out that wicked laugh again. "I don't like to get into a serious relationship with no boy right now. I just fool around."

"You don't take any of them seriously," I offered.

"They don't take any of me seriously, why should I?" she answered quickly. "They think I'm an easy girl. They just want me because some of the boys tell them that I do this, and I do it to them or whatever. Then I feel bad." She breaks off to laugh once more. "I'm so crazy. I want to change, but it's so difficult."

Though Maria has been restored to home, it's an uneasy peace. She hates her new school and is convinced that all the other girls—who are mostly black—are jealous of her. "It's so bad. I'm the only Latino there. My English is not that good—I have my accent. The girls, they jealous. If you have long hair, they, like, they hate you. You can't even look at them. They come up to your face: 'What you lookin' at me?' I can't do nothin'. The boys are so fresh." She makes a *phew*-noise of outrage. "They want to grab you, they want to do whatever with you. If you say no, they like, 'Man, why you actin' like that?'"

On weekends, Maria still sneaks out of her stepmother's house by leaving three pillows under the covers and climbing out the window. She goes to parties where she can flirt with boys, lose herself in what she knows and does best. But sometimes the fears, the darkness, will catch up with her. At night, she said, she dreams about getting pregnant. "I dreamt that I was already with this big, big belly and nobody wanted to help me." She made a noise in her throat; her hand flew to her mouth. "Oh God," she said with a gasp. "My father would kill me."

A year later I learned that Maria had completed her first year at community college. "Maria's tough," commented Sandra Canas, the community organizer Maria turned to when she was going through rough patches.

Hector

Eighteen years old

"I had no more choice. I stay here, I'll be a dead man."

When Hector came to the United States, he really immigrated into two countries. One country was in the tiled halls of school, where fellow immigrant students struggled to communicate in their ESL classes, bells clanged, strange kids jostled down the stairs to their next period. The other country was behind the stucco buildings and gated stores, on the streets, where guys in baggy pants hung around their souped-up cars. This country felt real. Its citizens welcomed him, gave him the survival skills he needed for America.

Though it's considered a poor neighborhood, to my eyes, the Belmont section of Los Angeles, where Hector lives, is pretty, set high on a hill and not far from the few tall buildings of downtown. On Belmont Avenue, former drive-in hamburger joints are now *taquerias* and Mexican fish houses, sporting bright, festive colors on their walls. Belmont High School is freshly painted and boasts a huge football field. The houses are well kept. But when I see the place through Hector's eyes, I start to see that, despite the palm trees and green lawns, it's a war zone divided between gangs.

A small, lively teenager with combed-back black hair and an open, eager face, Hector is very honest about his life. He has the freshly scrubbed, clear-eyed look of some-

Hector

one who's seen the worst and pulled himself up again. Now he's a poster boy for goodness, his plaid flannel shirt tucked neatly into his slacks, his schoolbooks carried under his arm. English trips off his tongue in his rush to tell his story, though he easily remembers what it was like not to know a word of the language.

Hector is a cheerful, no-nonsense guy, someone who doesn't have time for self-pity; who has always veered between being the good and the bad boy. Back in Guatemala City, his grandmother reared him, since his mother had already immigrated to the States. By the time he was twelve, he had dropped out of school and taken to wandering the streets for days, returning to his grandmother's home for a hot meal and sleep. This went on for three years, until Hector realized his life was going nowhere. He called his mother, who wired him money to come to Los Angeles. Hector set off, excited to make a fresh start, transform himself into a good boy all over again.

Los Angeles was a rude awakening. His mother worked long hours at night and was hardly around. He didn't know a word of English. He found himself at Belmont High School—a huge school filled with kids from all different backgrounds, which scared him. "People come from China, people from South America, and you don't know how those guys act," he explained. "How am I going to act to those guys? How am I going to have a conversation? I was so shy. I thought maybe I'm going to fail all my classes."

For all his shyness, Hector can't resist reaching out, talking to people. He searches for friendship and community wherever he goes. One way he made friends was through his hobby of coin collecting. Hector would introduce himself to the other immigrant students and ask each to give him a coin from his or her country. In this way, he began to piece together a world made of different parts. "I don't want to buy the coins. I just want to get them from somebody I know." And, he adds proudly, he got twenty-four coins in all.

But it was not enough. Hector was still lonely. Every night, while his mother worked, he was left alone in a small apartment. Once more, in his usual affable way, he reached out. On his way to the store one evening to buy some candy, he stopped to chat with the gang members who hung out on the corner. To his surprise, they didn't try to intimidate him or recruit him—at first. "They started to talk to me, where am I coming from, what is my name, and everything.

If you want to call me, just come here. You're not going to be a *cholo* [gangster], you just going to be friends and kicking around and things like that. And I say, Okay."

The first thing that impressed him was their English. "How did you learn English like that?" he asked.

"On the streets," they explained.

This other country, that of the streets, had a lot to offer him—survival skills and the warmth and intimacy he couldn't find at school. Since Hector didn't want to burden his mother with his problems, he began turning to the guys in the gang.

"I thought it was my family. They were like, I'm here for you. Every time I have a problem, I talk to them and they say, Don't worry about it, we can fix. I never told my mom. My mom had a lot of problems—rent, and food, send money to my little brothers. She has been working since she was sixteen. She has been working too much. I'm not going to give her more problems. My dad isn't my dad. I never talk to him. I don't know him. He's a good guy, but that's it. We don't usually talk about my problems."

Before he knew it, he was depending on the gang members for everything—advice, a sense of belonging. Even though he'd tried to stay good, the bad boy in him was reawakened, excited by the sense of danger. Hector was "jumped" into the gang, which means he proved himself by fighting off four or five other gang members. Now he was a bona-fide *cholo*. He was part of a nation, with its own codes and rituals for manhood and loyalty. He began to dress like a gangster, in baggy pants, his face an intimidating mask. There were fights, though only the "elders" in the gang carried guns. He stuck to knives.

"Being a gang member, you have to feel it," he explained. "You have to be something you are proud of being.

When you talking about your country, you say, I'm proud of my country. It's the same thing. You got to feel proud of the gangs."

His life filled out with parties and girlfriends. "I was going around with *cholitas* and started using drugs. Mostly marijuana. They like to drink and party. There were a lot of girls who got involved with sex and drugs and drinking. Now I can say this is not good. Then I was, This is cool, this is fun. That's exactly what I was looking for."

"Was it exciting?"

"It wasn't really exciting," he answered frankly. At first the bad boy in him thrilled to all the temptations he had once steered clear of—drugs, alcohol, smoking. His new gang country seemed to offer him freedom. But that freedom quickly soured when he spent two weeks in a juvenile-detention center for throwing rocks and beer bottles. "It was so boring," he admits.

One day Hector and a friend stopped to talk to a few girls on the street. Suddenly a Buick came screeching around the corner. The girls, as it turned out, were *cholitas* in a rival gang. Shots rang out. Hector watched as his closest friend—his big brother, really—crumpled to the pavement. Enraged, Hector grabbed stones, anything he could find, and tore after the speeding car, but it was no use. His friend lay dead on the ground. To this day, Hector can't even remember the color of the car or the face of the guy who'd shot his friend.

The police never followed up on the murders. "When a gangster is killed, the police don't care," Hector commented. "I think it's better for them. It's like, when you kill an insect, it's no more trouble. When you kill an insect or some other bad things, you kill a bacteria or something like that."

Hector's life began to fall apart. He was kicked out of school. He felt unhappy, but he wanted to stay loyal to the codes that had been handed down to him. One of those is a saying—"You got to be *truca.*" That means you have to watch with four eyes—two in the back, two in the front. One day, Hector wasn't *truca,* and he landed himself in deep trouble.

During a robbery, Hector's role was to play lookout and watch for cops so his fellow gang members could do their work. Then a friend came by, and Hector got so immersed in talking to him he didn't notice the cop cars. All the gang members were caught except for Hector, who managed to flee down the street.

Hector had saved his skin, but now his life was in danger. "In gangs, if you make a mistake, that's terrible," he said. "They started to make calls to different gangs that I did a mistake, and they want to kill me. I had no more choice. I stay here, I'll be a dead man."

His mother, who had since moved to New York, begged him to leave Los Angeles and join her. So he fled the city, stayed for a few weeks with an aunt in Queens, and then settled in at his mother's on Long Island. He was in hiding for about six months. But he didn't like it in New York. He found the city "crazy." And his heart was back on the streets of Los Angeles, where, for better or worse, he'd made his home. So he contacted the people he knew. As it turned out, many of the caught gang members had been sent back to their countries. The ones set on revenge were in trouble themselves with the gang leaders: they'd made their own mistakes. The way was clear. Hector could go home.

Except for one problem: he had no place to go. Hector called everyone he knew, but it was always the same story: no one wanted to live with a gang member—even a former gang member. He'd betrayed one citizenship for another.

No matter how much he'd straightened up, reclaimed the good boy in him, no one wanted the potential trouble. Then his mother called the cousin of Hector's stepfather, and he agreed to let Hector come stay with them. "He's like an uncle to me," Hector happily told me. "He's known me since I was a little kid."

This is where Hector lives now—in a two-story house on a pleasant street, with three grown men who share the downstairs apartment and a family in the upstairs apartment. Once again he's found a new family. They often eat and socialize together, keep an eye on one another. He has signed up for classes at the adult night school and gotten a job parking cars in a lot. And, in his usual outgoing way, he strolled into the Newcomers Center and asked if he could volunteer in the office.

One day, Maria Olmos, the director of the Newcomers Center at Belmont High School, noticed Hector and asked why he wasn't in regular classes. He told her his story and she cut a deal with him: if he would stop dressing like a gangster and start improving his attitude, she would see about his getting into day classes. They both kept the bargain, and Hector is enrolled in high school. Now he talks about graduation and becoming a community leader, helping teenagers of all backgrounds. His new life as a "good boy" has really begun.

He even has a new girlfriend—a Chicana girl—and on the day Hector and I met the second time, I spotted them walking together in the halls. She has a sweet, heart-shaped face and gently held his arm as he chivalrously escorted her to her locker and out of the building. Hector is clearly proud, but not boastful. He's also thoughtful about what his former life was like. When I ask him what the difference is between having a "regular" girlfriend and going out with the *cholitas,* he's very blunt:

"When you have a gangster girlfriend, it sounds so rude—they just like to go to bed, smoke, and do bad things. They *never, never, never* say 'I love you' or 'I like you.' It's hard for them to say 'I love you.' The girl that I'm going out with right now, she's, like, telling me every day, 'I really like you and I hope you change a lot and some day we get married.' She's almost seventeen; if I finish high school, maybe someday we can get married. That's what I like from the other girls. It's about the future."

Ironically, since Hector's return, the gang leaders keep an eye on him to make sure he doesn't come back to their ways. When he goes to visit them, they scold him. "What are you doing here?" they want to know. "Go back home. You've got to go to school. You've got to graduate." They're still his big brothers, but they're watching him from the other side.

It's not just that Hector has returned to his good-boy self. All along, he was looking for the same thing—belonging, friendship, comfort. Hector is a sensible guy who has been on a journey there and back; who knows how to get off when the road he's on turns bleak and self-destructive. He knows what it's like to live inside a different country.

As we finished our talk and headed toward the car, I noticed his sense of freedom, a light bounce in his step. I drove him home, and he pointed out the different grafitti scrawled on the walls, which ones belonged to which gang. He identified a group going into a liquor store. Against the wide Los Angeles boulevards, the huge sky, everyone looked tiny. But through Hector's eyes I saw how these gang members make their mark on the landscape, carve out their own country.

Hector learned that this other country was a trap, a place with no passport out. There were only more fights and robberies and parties. He couldn't get in an elevator without seeing the passengers flinch in fear. He couldn't hang around a shopping mall without being shadowed by cops. He couldn't get through school without getting kicked out. And though this other country helped him bridge his past and present, there was no way into a future. Hector has lived in both countries, and he's survived to tell about it.

"Ana"

Seventeen years old

I was raised by my grandmother in Mexico. Then my mother in Los Angeles sent for me. When I came over here to California, my mother started hitting me right away. She had gotten married to another man. When she drank, she would say I was with her husband. She was jealous of me.

After four months, she told me to leave. The night my mother kicked me out of the house, in front of where we lived there was a big gang. They could do anything to me. The streets are not safe. I went to my mother's friend and she helped me.

When I left home, my mother's husband left too. My mother thought I was with her husband. She came to her friend's house to look for him. When she didn't find him, she started to hit me. My mother's friend reported her to the police.

I've been eight months in a foster home, a shelter with other girls. I like the shelter and am friends with the other girls. One is from Guatemala, one is from Mexico, the other is from Peru. I don't want a relationship with my mother. My mother prefers her husband more than me.

Reshmee

Seventeen years old

> *"My father says that when he eats, he's eating his own blood. I make his heart bleed so much because I disrespect him."*

For several months, Reshmee led a secret life. Instead of going to school, she took the train from her home in Jersey City to the World Trade Center in Manhattan. There she made her way up the escalator to the Borders Bookstore café. The security guard, who came to recognize her, always waved in greeting. She bought herself something to drink, then sat for hours, stared out the plate-glass window, and made up stories about the people walking in the streets below. She did anything to forget who she was, forget her life on the other side of the river.

Tamila—or Reshmee, as she calls herself—speaks softly but intensely, as if is she has been waiting for this interview all her life, waiting to tell her story. And perhaps I have been waiting too. My father is also from Guyana, and I was curious about a girl who partly shared my background.

In some ways, a Guyanese identity is the ultimate "remix." It is not pure but rather a fusion of other immigrations. In the nineteenth century, people from India came to this small country on the tip of South America to work the sugar plantations. In moving halfway across the globe, groups from different regions and castes mingled; no one was really sure who came from where. That is the

Reshmee

beauty and pain of immigration: it shakes up the old roles that people are locked into.

In Guyana, the Indian coolies lived side by side with recently freed slaves from Africa. A tentative Creole culture was created—in the foods, the patois dialect, the village life, where a Presbyterian church might be down the road from a Hindu temple. Unfortunately, over time, the country split along racial lines. Once again there an upheaval, and in the past two decades, huge numbers of Guyanese have streamed to the United States, Canada, and England.

Here in the States, Indo-Guyanese don't fit any clear spot on the racial and ethnic map. Many move into neighborhoods where they're mistaken for being Hispanic and just blend in. Others live in neighborhoods such as Richmond Hill, Queens, where they can walk down the street and hear pounding chutney-calypso music, pick up a roti-and-curry meal, and read the latest news from home. In the United States, Guyanese are often looked down upon by those from India, who do not regard them as "authentic." At the same time, many quickly want to become "Yankee" as a way of forgetting their politically troubled homeland.

Reshmee was born in a small village in Guyana, not far from where my own father grew up, and emigrated with her family when she was a year old. She is a tall, big-boned girl, her hair is streaked a light tan, and her fingers flash with several rings. She visited Guyana a few times when she was growing up, and the people there would always greet her as if she'd left just the other day. Guyana is like a small town that keeps an eye on its own.

"When I was little, I was the only Guyanese girl, so I really didn't know what it was to be Guyanese. I took a step back and I didn't like what I saw. I saw somebody who wanted to be like everybody else. I saw myself dressing the way they were. I saw myself saying I didn't have a religion, since most of my friends were Christian. I didn't understand what Hinduism was. I didn't know who I was anymore. I felt like, when I looked at myself in the mirror, I was trying to be one of them.

"The teachers used to ask questions, 'Tamila, what's it like in Guyana?' And I'd be like, 'I don't know.' 'Tamila, why do they wear Indian clothes when you're from Guyana?' And I have no idea. I'm, like, Okay, this isn't making any sense. Everybody else can talk about who they are, where they're from. They can trace back their great-grandfathers who were born in Jersey City. I didn't have that. I didn't know anything. I felt as if I had no identity. I was no one."

As she talked, I could hear how urgently she wanted to "be someone," to seize hold of something that would place her. This was a common teenage yearning and a desire to find her roots. It also was a portrait of a twice-displaced people, who have tried to hold on to who they are over several generations and homes.

In Reshmee's case, she also had something else to overcome: her father. Clearly, Reshmee loves her father and is very proud of him. A self-made immigrant who came to the country with fifty dollars in his pocket, he has worked his way up as an emergency-medical nurse to support his family. He is especially generous with her; he recently bought her a new computer and always makes sure she has everything she needs. But Reshmee's father has a darker side: he drinks, and has fathered children outside the family. "I think, because he's been drinking so long, the alcohol has eaten away his mind," she comments. This is the shadow Reshmee has grown up under—her father's decline, his reputation—and it has driven her to succeed, stand out, and prove herself. She is obsessed with being good, and keeps repeating how she wants to be a "good" person, doing good for people.

So the unsettled Guyanese girl plunged into her new-found Indianness. She switched from using the name "Tamila" to "Reshmee." She read books about Hinduism, and learned the story of her great-grandparents, who came from the province of Uttar Pradesh and the city of Delhi to the Caribbean. To her, the most exciting revelation was the news that her family was Brahmin, or high-caste.

"It was so cool. My father to me, said, 'We're Brahmin.' And I said, 'What's the difference between Brahmin?' He was like, 'You're the highest caste.' I didn't know. I was like, 'Oh, that's so interesting.' I never really thought of myself as being a person that's in the hierarchy."

"What do you like about it?" I asked.

"I like being different from anybody else. I was so deprived of who I was—to finally have something to be. I have something to be, and the whole culture, it's mine, it belongs to me, it's what I am, it's what make me be what I am."

This fascination with being Brahmin made me uncomfortable. When people emigrated from India, the caste system was shattered. I used to be told the same story about my family in Guyana, that they were Brahmin until they converted to Christianity. These tales of India are what many Guyanese tell each other, the nostalgic stories that heal the break with the past.

When my father came to this country years ago, he too went through an identity crisis. He was attending a black university in Washington, D.C., which was then a Jim Crow city, where whites and blacks were starkly segregated. He didn't fit into any neat racial or ethnic categories. He threw himself into an Indian world and decided to work for the Indian consulate. To be connected to India helped fill in the gaps in his own self, and allowed him to understand the customs and attitudes that were carried on by his family in the Caribbean. It also let him be part of a grand civilization rather than the "little palm tree, little road village" that he was so ashamed of. Reaching backward to a culture he never quite knew was a way to make his difficult transition into the future.

Similarly, in her newfound identity, Reshmee watched Indian movies and taught herself how to do Indian dances and sing traditional songs. The kids from India made fun of her. "The Indian people in my school say, 'You're not Indian, you're not supposed to be dancing an Indian song. You're supposed to be dancing a Guyanese song.' I'm not going to do calypso-chutney, I'm going to dance a nice Indian song, because I can do it. Apparently I'm not Indian enough. I'm telling you, my grandmother, my great-grandfather, they're from India, apparently that makes me a descendant from India. I was just born in Guyana. Don't I look Indian?"

Reshmee grew ever more active in the local Guyanese temple and appeared as a classical dancer at Guyanese weddings. This caused ripples in the community. Gossip began to swirl around her. To Reshmee, the other girls were jealous because, with no training at all, she was excelling at what they had labored over for years.

"I love to dance. I started to dance in shows, at weddings, and when I danced I guess I was a little too good. And the girls started saying things about me. I also taught myself to sing traditional singing. And I started singing in the church. People, they didn't like it because they were singing for years. They didn't want me there anymore. The guys started knowing who I was. Then they found out who my father was. So apparently if the father does it the daughter does it too."

Classical dancing, which for Indian girls is like ballet lessons for American girls, suddenly took on a sexual and taboo meaning. "I was seen as a whore. That's what people called me. I really don't think I am a whore, and I think I'm a pretty good person. Dancing is my passion, and it's something I do because I love."

Reshmee had shown tremendous will in teaching herself traditional singing and dancing. Yet Indian classical forms—dance, music, singing—require years and years of training. They are a tradition that demands obedience to a guru, a master. To Reshmee, classical dance and singing was an outlet for her personal expression, her craving to be seen and appreciated, to mark herself as Indian.

More and more stories circulated about Reshmee. When her father went to a bar, he'd hear rumors that Reshmee was sleeping with boys. Driven wild with suspicions, Reshmee's father began to accuse her of doing drugs and sleeping around. He forbade her to sing at the temple. Her mother believed her husband was possessed by a demon, and she even went to an obeah woman to see if they could cast a spell. Reshmee knew that drink was behind these rageful episodes.

"It hurts, because he believes them. I'm like, Dad, don't you know your daughter? I've been living here my whole life; don't you know me by now?"

"He says, 'I really don't know you, because I don't know what people tell me.' My father says that when he eats, he's eating his own blood. I make his heart bleed so much because I disrespect him."

To an outsider, her father's accusations sound absurd, for Reshmee seems like the model daughter. Yet, in some ways, like any teenager, Reshmee *was* a stranger to her father. When a parent says, 'I don't know you,' it's also because his or her little son or daughter has erupted into an unrecognizable person. Reshmee was growing up, dressing like a young woman, dancing for strangers, having her own opinions. Her drive to be noticed, to be special, seemed dangerous to her father, no matter how well intentioned or innocent. A girl who preens and dances publicly can quickly be shamed in the Guyanese community. And the more Reshmee wanted to shine in public, the more disturbed he grew. To rise was also to be exposed. Reshmee's father gave in to his own fears, his knowledge of his own weaknesses, and envisioned the worst—his daughter's downfall.

"He thought I'm getting too known. If more people know you, there's more people to destroy you," she said.

The rumors were flying fast and furious now. One of the Guyanese boys Reshmee liked was a computer hacker who accessed her account, stole her father's credit-card number, and charged things, claiming Reshmee had done it. Then he threatened to ruin her life if she didn't sleep with him. When she refused, he called up Reshmee's father and told him she was pregnant.

"My father believed everything. He came into my room at three o'clock in the morning. He was like, 'I don't know who you are, you're not my daughter. You're probably just a whore.' "

By the morning, Reshmee had fled the house. For two days, "the longest days of my life," Reshmee wandered around, not sure what to do. She spent time at a friend's house, but was disgusted by the sight of a mother and son smoking together. In the meantime, the whole family—all the aunts and uncles and cousins—came together "like a wake." Her mother used a pager to beg Reshmee to come home. It was only when her father broke down crying and admitted that he missed her that she returned.

It was not the same. Her father could not forgive her for leaving. "It was like I didn't have a father for a long time. He said I wasn't his daughter anymore when I left." And so many accusations and rumors had finally left their mark; Reshmee began to doubt herself. Was she all those things everyone said she was?

Reshmee, the hardworking student, cheerful joiner of cultural clubs, began to cut school. Her parents knew something was wrong; her father was sure Reshmee was sneaking off to see a guy. But she was at the Borders café in Manhattan. Every day she took the train into the city and sat at the window, staring out at the people. She wrote stories in her notebook. "I pushed away all my friends, my family, I went into my own little world. And I stared out and put myself in other people's lives." The downfall her father feared had indeed come. She was flunking out of school.

Finally, the school called up her house and got her back on track through a home-instruction program. Reshmee more or less returned to her old life, though the hurt from the past year still lingers. She is upset about what the Guyanese community has done to her, and she keeps them at a wary distance.

At the same time, this experience has propelled her outward, away from the community that sabotaged her. All along, Reshmee had slowly found herself through a very different community: her magnet school, where kids of all backgrounds defined themselves by succeeding and aiming for college. It was in school that she began to see a way out, into the future.

"I love my school," she told me. "People there don't put me down. It's like, once I walk in there, everything else is obsolete. I'm not Guyanese, I'm not the girl who does this or that. I'm not known as the girl who talks to a lot of guys. I'm just Tamila."

Without telling her parents, Reshmee secretly applied to the University of Miami for early admission to their premed program. One day a letter arrived. Hands trembling, she opened the letter and started to cry.

"What's going on?" her mother asked.

"I've been accepted to the University of Miami," she whispered.

"You're not going," her mother said. "It's too far away."

Her parents were furious. Her father, angry that she had made a decision without his approval, did not speak to her for weeks.

"My father wanted me to go to Syracuse or somewhere near here, so when he puts his hand out he could grab me back. He wanted to be there if I fall, he could see it. Or if I need help, he's there. He wants to be a father. In Miami, he can't know what I'm doing. I think I wanted it that way. I wanted to show him that I could take it on myself."

When we first spoke, Reshmee was still fighting with her parents over her decision. Reshmee was so determined to go that she told them she would pay for it herself, through student loans. Her father was finally relenting, though the troubles between them remain complicated and contradictory.

"I'm so much like him. He doesn't want me to fall. He doesn't want me to do all the bad things that he did. He wants me to be somebody, but he's scared. He's expecting me to fall. He's expecting me to say, I'm going to go to college and I'm going to bring home a baby. I know for myself I'm going to be a doctor. I'm going to bring home a degree, I'm going to take care of his grandchildren. I will be somebody someday. I have a lot of dreams and I'm going to make them true. Because I think I deserve that."

After our interview was over, I left to go uptown. I had a pounding headache, and went to my husband's office to lie down. My headache exploded into a migraine. *He's eating his own blood.* I could hear the curses, the violence of their feelings toward one another. Guyana, the darkness, the sense of failure. The dreaded feeling that you might be pulled back into the past; that you can't leave the past behind. All of this I knew through my own father, who wished the best for his American children but also feared that the worst might befall us.

In Guyana, they talk about family curses, but it is also another way of saying how our parents' pasts, their cultures, mark us. In every family there is a push and pull, a desire to push the child out of the warm circle of family, and a desire to keep him or her close. Then there is the shocking moment when a kid reaches his teenage years. To the parents, their teenager is both out of their control and eerily familiar. The parents are staring at an earlier version of themselves all over again, with their own weaknesses. And for an immigrant parent, how much of the past will shape and damage this newly formed person, nurtured in a different country, different soil and air?

Reshmee's days cutting classes, wandering the streets, brought me back to my own teen years when I had gone from being a high-achieving student to cutting most of my classes. In my family I was both encouraged and held back, kept near to home. Like Reshmee, I understood that fine line in adolescence, where you are struggling with who you are while your parents are sinking under their own demons. That can be the moment that breaks or strengthens you: It is the end of romance about your parents, the end of nostalgia. You realize that your parents are limited, and that only you, as a half-formed adult, know what's best for you. Only you can be the keeper of your own stories, your own life.

When Reshmee and I last met, she was flushed and excited. Her parents had finally agreed to let her go to Miami, and they had already traveled to a special orientation on the campus. She chatted about the campus, the classes, the warm tropical city with palm trees. Finally, the world was opening up to her. To me, this seemed the most solid of

Reshmee's searches for herself, more than the dance, the singing, the change in her name. Finally, she wasn't the girl in Jersey City, the Guyanese girl trying to be Indian, the good daughter accused of being bad. Another immigration was about to happen, to another city. Another remix, another chance.

The Americas, the New World, are all about mixtures; it's a shattering and a coming together. It's a remix. We tell stories, we hear stories. We listen to the voices in this book, the mingled hum of lives shattering and fusing again. Listen to Hector—good boy, bad boy, gang boy, schoolboy again. Or Yulia, half California adolescent, half wise Russian woman; Sorianyi, survivor for a woman halfway across the world; Nubaisha, proud daughter of a Pakistani major learning to fight back American-style; Mari, learning to look people in the eye; Herman, mixing and remixing reggae and pop. We are broken and we make ourselves whole again. We remix the old and we make ourselves new.

Index